THE TEFLON®
GUIDE TO
NOT GETTING
STUCK IN
THE KITCHEN

THE TEFLON® GUIDE TO
NOT GETTING STUCK IN THE KITCHEN

by SYLVIA SCHUR
drawings by Isadore Seltzer
CORINTHIAN EDITIONS, Inc.
New York   1969

Library of Congress Catalog Card Number: 77-81774
Manufactured in the United States of America

Contents

1
How to plan a new kitchen or remodel an old one

2
How to equip a modern kitchen

3
How to shop a supermarket

4
How to store foods—how to freeze

THE TEFLON® GUIDE TO NOT GETTING STUCK IN THE KITCHEN

Chapter 1

How to plan a new kitchen or remodel an old one

Since man first learned to treasure fire, ringing it with stones to preserve a blaze, the place where food is prepared has been the social center of the family. In ancient Rome, Vesta the goddess of fire watched over the life of every home. Her sacred kitchen shrine, the focus of home life, was carefully tended.

Here in America, as we harnessed our natural resources to make a constant source of heat and energy available to all, a new goddess was born—the goddess of efficiency. Until fairly recently her shrine was a kitchen of pristine white, with rigid placement of white appliances and equipment, where American women came to feel exiled in sterile laboratories.

Today new freedom in kitchen design is responsible for the emergence of an emancipated woman in the kitchen, one with an experience of a wide world of foods and dishes, possessing a whole range of technological skills for turning out complicated meals quickly and easily—and a genius for cleaning up afterward.

Whether you are planning a brand new kitchen or remodeling an old one, there has never been a more exciting time for developing this, the core of your home, into a pleasant, functional place to be. Today, at last, you can create your own highly personal environment for food preparation—where the name of the game is enjoyment.

Free yourself of the confining image of a room with four walls in front of which your appliances stand amid scattered segments of counter. Now you can think of your kitchen as a grouping of defined areas in which a number of specific operations occur.

- The storage of foods.
- The preparation of these foods into meals.
- The refrigeration and freezing of foods.
- The boiling, braising, broiling, and baking of foods.
- The cleaning center, both for preliminary preparation of foods and for wash-up and refuse disposal afterward.
- People centers for planning household operations, for serving light meals, for social communication.
- Special areas such as a pet center, or a playpen center, or a handweaving center with a loom, if these are the things *you* do in your kitchen.
- Ventilation, for improving the function of cooking, as well as for general comfort.
- Lighting to see all this clearly.
- Decorating to enhance kitchen life itself.

But first let us speak of function. Are you slave to an outmoded kitchen? Are you wasting time and effort with every meal you prepare, taking too long with every pan you wash?

Saving time and emotions

By adapting principles discovered in highly scientific time-and-motion research you can probably cut your kitchen time in half. To do so you may have to consider rearranging your appliances and kitchen equipment for more efficient use.

By following simple principles of food selection and storage, perhaps you can cut meal preparation time in half—and eat better than ever, shop less often and save 20 percent or more on your marketing. By using cookware coated with Teflon you can eliminate many chores, such as scouring pots and pans.

As much as any room in the house, your kitchen can reflect your taste and individuality in arrangement, in color, and in the selection of equipment and appliances, even when your plan for your new or remodeled kitchen emphasizes function. Efficiency studies prove that the time-and-motion principles that increase profitability in business can work for you, too, and save you money. While your actual dollar savings may be smaller than those in industry, the percentage of change is likely to be larger.

Calculated on the basis of $2.50 an hour, the wage of an office worker of moderate skill, a homemaker who spends four and a half hours in the kitchen seven days a week, plus four hours a week shopping, would earn $88.40 a week. This does not include pay for house cleaning, laundry or other related tasks, which would account for five hours, or $12.50, more. The homemaker's seven-day week is then worth almost $101. Assuming she takes a two-week vacation, this adds up to more than $5,000 a year. If kitchen and housework could be reduced by half, such savings would have a $2,500 monetary value, aside from the preserved energy and well-being of the worker on this job. Putting a dollar figure on the value of the time saved, almost any new kitchen installation can be "amortized" in a year!

A 3,000-mile hike

If you were to undergo a time-and-motion analysis of your kitchen tasks, a pedometer would be hung on your belt to measure the miles you walk. The figures would probably startle you. It is not unusual for a housewife to walk 3,000 miles a year, the equivalent of hiking all the way from New York to California!

Tests show that rearranging a kitchen can cut steps in the preparation and serving of breakfast from 500 to 200 steps; from 700 to 200 for preparing and serving dinner; from 600 to 150 steps for washing the dinner dishes. Rearranging a kitchen can cut cooking and cleanup time by as much as one-third, but even more dramatic changes can be made by taking advantage of the benefits of a full range of food and housekeeping products. Principles of efficiency extend even into the methods of storage; lifting a load above shoulder height adds 25 percent of the weight of the worker to the weight of the object. Lifting a load from the floor to a table adds 40 percent of the body weight to the weight of the object being lifted. The goal of energy saving is to create an energy reserve for meeting other family and personal needs and thus providing happier, more carefree living.

The satisfaction felt with a job well done in the time available is directly related to the actual time-and-motion saving involved. You can achieve the same satisfaction in the meals you prepare, using far fewer steps and motions by coupling a conscious awareness of time-and-motion efficiency with the most effective use of modern appliances, equipment, and utensils. Which would you rather do? Make 50 tearful up-and-down rubs on a grater to grate an onion or whirl it to shreds in a blender? Would you rather walk to one closet for salt, another for flour, and a third for shortening, or reach for all three in a convenient range-side cabinet?

Many of the steps in the preparation of a meal require a number of stops and starts before the meal can be completed. You save time if the foods, supplies, and equipment for each job are grouped close together. Modern homemakers who freeze dishes for future meals require additional work space, with wrapping materials close at hand. Food freezing contributes to more varied meals and to a sense of security because you will be able to cope with unplanned-for meal needs and unexpected guests.

A well-organized kitchen helps you create meals in less time and with less effort. Whether your kitchen is only a corner of an apartment or a big friendly room in which children and friends gather, it is important to plan the major traffic routes. If there will be visitors in your kitchen, allow for a place where they can sit and talk or help stir a batter. If the man in your family does the grilling, or fancies himself as a pastry chef, plan centers for his activities.

When you plan a new kitchen, it's a good idea to talk it over with the members of your family. You may find that your son has some clever ideas about equipment and its placement or that your daughter has some useful suggestions about cleanup. You will be encouraging an awareness of kitchen efficiency in your family as you work out the details.

Cooking style and kitchen style

Your particular style and pattern of cooking count heavily in planning a kitchen for saving time. If you customarily use foods largely prepared before they reach the kitchen, you might want to emphasize the freezer and quick-heating facilities. If you are an ardent home baker, a double oven should be in your plan. If grilled foods are your speciality, you will want to accommodate a good grill in your kitchen and an effective venting arrangement. Most kitchens combine a variety of special functions like these. Whatever your final plan, the concept of efficiency is the same: plan centers for major kitchen activities, with best access for each function and efficient easy flow between the centers.

Organize work centers according to your needs. If you do much baking, plan on a mixing center complete with mixer and bowls, rolling pin, baking pans, measuring spoons, spatula, and cups. Store the flour, leavening, flavoring, shortening, sugars, food coloring, nuts, chocolate, raisins, and waxed paper close by. Install a work surface appropriate for rolling out pastry—wood, marble, or sheet plastic. Keep a stool handy so you won't have to stand while beating a mix or decorating a cake.

The seven basic centers

For consistently efficient meal preparation, you should consider seven basic centers for the various aspects of food storage, meal preparation, and cleanup:

- *Food-preparation center* for assembling ingredients, mixing foods, and wrapping prepared foods until time for use.
- *Sink center* to provide water and drainage for food

preparation and cleanup. This should also include storage facilities for dishwashing supplies and equipment and a rubbish-disposal area. You will need counters to the right and left of the sink, to provide space for preparing food or for dirty dishes on one side and clean-rinsed dishes on the other. If possible to install, a second source of water in the kitchen will be very convenient, either at a double sink or, better still, at an auxiliary sink in another part of the kitchen. The sink center is the most-used work area in any kitchen. It must function perfectly.

- *Cooking center* with burners for surface cooking, an oven for baking and roasting, a broiler, and possibly a griddle and a grill. These cooking functions may be assembled in a single unit or separated for greater efficiency. Surface cooking units are used far more often than baking or grilling units.
- *Cold center* for refrigeration of perishable foods and freezer storage of frozen foods or the freezing of foods procured or prepared for later use.
- *Small-appliance center* placed near where unit will be used most often. Or these appliances may be individually placed—can opener near the cabinet where canned foods are stored; bottle opener near the refrigerator where cold drinks are chilled; mixer and blender near the food-preparation center.
- *Pots-and-pans center* near the food-preparation and range area.
- *Tableware center* for the storage of equipment for serving and dining, placed close to the sink and in a path to the dining area.

The kitchen triangle

In planning these areas, remember that you will be moving often from sink to refrigerator, from sink to range, and from range to refrigerator. The kitchen traffic triangle may be laid out as a literal triangle with straight unobstructed "paths" between sink and refrigerator, between sink and range, and between range and refrigerator. The kitchen triangle can be laid out efficiently in a kitchen of any shape. For greatest efficiency the sides of the triangle should measure:

> Four to seven feet between sink and refrigerator
> Four to six feet between sink and range
> Four to nine feet between range and refrigerator

Equipment can be placed to form a triangle for work flow in a kitchen of any space. Here are five basic plans:

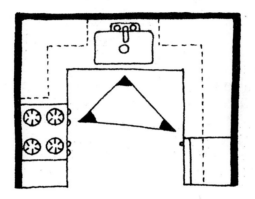

The U-shaped kitchen provides the best traffic and work pattern. A compact work triangle is easy to fit into this arrangement, the sink area forming the point of the triangle for step saving.

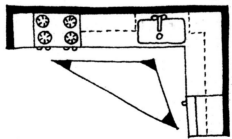

The L-shaped kitchen can be set up in almost any adequate space. For greatest efficiency, consider putting the cooking section of the L closest to the dining area, the refrigeration section closest to where food is prepared for storing. This plan works well in a square room.

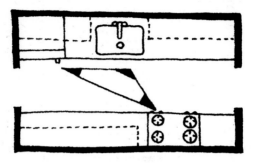

The corridor kitchen, in which equipment is lined up on two facing walls, can be designed to save steps in moving from one center to another. It is effective in a long, narrow room, provided that the kitchen area is at least 8 feet wide.

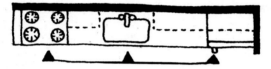

The one-wall kitchen makes the most of a narrow room, but is generally limited in storage and counter facilities. With such an arrangement consider using pull-out counter shelves, lazy-susan cabinet arrangements, wall-hung shelves, magnets and brackets for knives and equipment, to help utilize all available space.

The design-your-own-island kitchen is suitable for any large open room. Peninsulas jutting out into the room can double the counter space in your kitchen and serve as room dividers, setting off eating areas. Islands provide extra storage and counter space, and can be planned to incorporate a sink or a cook-top; surface cut-outs with removal inserts for easy rubbish disposal; drawers for utensil storage; a drop-leaf for serving; a roll-out cart for small appliances; file drawers for reference or other storage— all in the line with individual needs. The top surface may be Formica, or tile for handy pan set-down, or include a kitchen block surface and/or a marble insert for pastry-making. Be sure

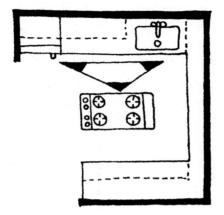

to allow enough walk-around room between any island and other equipment—36 inches is the recommended minimum.

Try to visualize your own patterns of movement before planning the placement of your major work centers. When you come in with packages from the market, where will you set them down? Where will you clean foods and dishes? Where will you store nonperishables (close to the place where they will eventually be used)? Where will you place foods for loading in refrigerator and freezer? Prepare foods for cooking? Cook? Carve? Serve? Plan the placement of work centers to enable you to have straight-line traffic routes between those used in sequence—you'll save many steps every day.

Planning your work centers

In planning each work center, think through all the functions you want it to serve. Then provide for:

- Its major appliance
- Auxiliary appliances and implements
- Work surface for preparation
- Storage and supplies used for the work center's particular function

Like a commander planning a military campaign, first think through the strategy for what you intend to accomplish in each center—the major appliance and how it will be used. Then select the tactics to reach your goal—the auxiliary appliances, equipment, supplies and their uses.

The sink center

This is a good place to start long-range remodeling or a new kitchen plan because it is the most used center. Sinks are available in enamel or stainless steel, and even in decorative ceramic. The latter is an elegant luxury more decorative than practical. Enamel sinks are the budget buy, easy to clean and generally practical, though subject to surface scratching and chipping. Stainless sinks are long-lasting, chip-proof. Where space is available, a double sink speeds food preparation and cleanup; one side may also be used for refuse-disposal installation. Check the range of sink styles, including corner models, to take best advantage of the space available to you.

- Check sink height installation for your convenience. Height of sink rim should reach 2 to 3 inches below elbow height of the person who uses the sink most often.
- Faucets with foot and knee pedals offer new convenience, freeing both hands for work. A spray-hose attachment speeds vegetable washing, dish rinsing, and sink cleaning. A soap insert included in some sprays may be valuable if there is no dishwasher, but is a questionable convenience where the hose is used most often for rinsing.
- For economy, back up kitchen plumbing to bathroom, if possible.
- Place the sink center between refrigerator and range centers for ideal flow of motion.
- Where possible, place the sink under a window—it's the most practical spot in the kitchen and good for the soul of the dish washer, an important consideration in kitchen efficiency.
- Allow 24 inches of space adjacent to sink cabinet for a dishwasher installation (on the right side if you are right-handed; on the left side for southpaws).

- Allow 36 inches of counter space to right of sink.
- Allow 30 inches of counter space to left of sink.
- Provide storage for all items that are first used at or near the sink, either for food preparation with water or for cleanup. This includes soaps, scouring powder and pads, brushes, towel racks, refuse-disposal bags, and can.
- If toddlers or pets are likely to explore the storage area under the sink, secure the doors with a sturdy latch.
- Plan a cutting-board surface near the sink, for ease of movement from washing to cutting foods.
- Place a multiple dispenser for paper towels, foil, plastic wrap, waxed paper, near sink.
- Keep a supply of glasses and/or paper or plastic cups near the sink for drinking.
- A second sink is a joy in the kitchen—for cleaning vegetables, arranging flowers, or soaking pans while the prime sink is in use. This sink may be smaller, perhaps round, and placed closer to the serving area, handy for providing water for the table or bar, as well as other uses.

The range center

Your cooking units may be incorporated in one entity, or installed separately for surface cooking, baking, grilling.

- Working surface should be 32 to 34 inches high for built-in top burners, unless you are unusually tall. The built-in oven should be placed so that the edge of the door, when opened down, is 5 to 7 inches below your elbow. Since

CLEANING TIPS: To clean broiler pan: If pan is Teflon-lined, simply pour off drippings and fat, then wash thoroughly in sudsy water. Pour off fat before it congeals, then allow pan to cool before cleaning it. With paper towels, wipe off excess fat from bottom of pan and from rack. Wash in hot, sudsy water, top burners are used far more frequently than the oven, their placement in a central position in the kitchen is far more important. If the oven is a separate unit, it can be placed against a far wall, out of the way.

- Provide adequate ventilation (exhaust fan) and adequate light for the cooking center. These functions may be combined in a ventilating hood with built-in light. Some models now include such niceties as a dish-warming rack and hooks for overhead hanging of utensils used at the range.
- Plan a food-preparation and cutting surface near the range.
- Consider a counter insert of heatproof material, such as stainless steel or tile, next to the range.
- Allow 24 inches next to the oven for setting down pans or servings.
- Provide cabinet space near the range for saucepans, skillets, cooking equipment, measuring utensils, ladles.
- Place cooking center on the route to the dining area, if that is convenient, but also consider that it is more convenient to have the cooking center near the sink.

The refrigeration center

Refrigeration and freezing units are separate entities, with separate doors if true freezing and adequate frozen-food storage are desired. In single units, decide whether you prefer the freezer over or under the refrigerator unit or in a side-by-side arrangement. Since the refrigerator is opened most often, having the refrigerator on top saves stooping. However, some homemakers prefer to have the refrigerator rather than the freezer accessible to small fry, and choose the freezer-on-top model. Side-by-side refrigerator-freezers generally offer greater capacity, but storage of large items or filled platters is limited in the freezer area. For maximum storage space, separate refrigerator and freezer units are offered in paired models, designed to stand side by side. The original chest-type top-loading freezer is now largely displaced in home use. Despite its economy, it was in-

FREEZER HINT: Just as with other foods, rotate frozen foods on a first-in, first-out basis. Put new packages at the back or the bottom of the freezer.

convenient for storage and access to foods. Both freezer and refrigerator can be installed with the doors flush with the surrounding wall, but do not adopt this remodeling program unless you have the space and ventilation (for the motor) behind the wall.

Allied with refrigerator or freezer, consider an ice-making attachment, a minor addition with major convenience in everyday living, which more than earns back the installation of a separate water line. Or evaluate the miracle of a microwave oven, now available for less than $500 for rapid cooking or reheating of frozen foods. These units cut your kitchen hours to about ten minutes.

- If freezer and refrigerator are placed side by side, install them so that the refrigerator, which is used more often, is closer to the work area.
- Allow a minimum of 18 inches work space adjacent to the refrigerator and freezer. A rolling work table is handy for this, since it can be wheeled to other sections of the room for loading. If this area is combined with the food-preparation center, allow 36 to 42 inches work space.
- Keep bottle opener, butter dishes, cream pitchers, ice-cream scoop, wrapping materials, storage dishes at hand close to this center.

The eating center

Large kitchen or small, there is something special about an easy meal served here in the heart of the home. Plan the eating area according to the intended scope of the room and your own meal patterns. A ledge for breakfast or quick meals suits the family with children; a small table with pull-up chairs meets the needs of a retired couple who enjoy a cup of tea in the afternoon. Whatever the design, these are basic requirements for comfort:

- Allow 24 inches of elbow room per person.
- Try to keep at least 2½ feet of clearance around the edge of the table.
- A minimum depth of 15 inches for your eating counter is adequate for breakfast—24 inches or more for dinner.
- Plan your table and seating equipment to meet the needs of those who will eat in the kitchen—tall, sturdy chairs for youngsters, a comfortable chair for father.
- For charm in the eating center, add a colorful centerpiece of fresh vegetables, a few flowers, a favorite print; polish an old copper kettle and fill it with wild grass from the side of the road, or grow your own chives in a pot.

The planning center

Set up your own niche for meal planning—a hanging shelf, a small table or desk, a chair with an attached arm, or a flush door atop two file cabinets. Your "kitchen office" will bring comfort as well as competence to meal planning.

- Place your phone here—on a long cord, so that you can carry it with you to stir a pan, if necessary.
- Keep your cookbooks here.
- Add pencils and paper for planning.
- Post a list of "most-called" and emergency numbers.
- Use a notebook or file for menus and guest lists.
- Set up a file drawer for your kitchen accounts and records.
- File equipment use-and-care manuals and guarantees here.

Watch this as an area of innovation for future use. If you hang your phone on the wall for lack of space now, and take notes on a pad clipped alongside it, plan for an expansion of this area in any remodeling. The "picture phone" of the future may enable you to dial a view of your supermarket and order by computer charge card inserted in your phone, right there in your own kitchen planning center!

Tools at hand

You save time and effort each time you tackle a kitchen task if supplies and equipment are ready and waiting for you. Organization of equipment reduces your kitchen mileage and saves effort in meal preparation through smooth flow of work. It pays to have "doubles" of some small tools such as knives and measuring utensils at various separate work centers in your kitchen.

Work is simplified if you store supplies and utensils where you use them *first*. This applies to storage at each of the kitchen counters. Keep mixing bowls where you can most handily pick them up to begin cooking; store skillets and saucepans that need preheating near the cooking center; those in which foods are first assembled near the preparation center. Plan a complete meal, insofar as you can, so that all the tasks at each center are accomplished in sequence, beginning with the preparation that will take the longest to complete. Dovetail motions wherever possible.

Plan work surfaces

Choose work surfaces to meet specific kitchen needs. Today counter tops come in a variety of materials and in many colors. You may wish to combine types of work surfaces to utilize the best features of each.

Durable and practical laminated plastics are fairly resistant to wear and abrasion. These come in many colors, patterns, and wood-grain finishes to match cabinets. While they are sturdy for normal use, they are marred by very hot pans, and scratch if they are used for cutting. A resilient surface such as heavy linoleum is inexpensive and will cut down on noise as well as breakage, but scratches and scorches in use. A stainless-steel top is expensive, but indestructible, easy to clean, and won't

MAKESHIFT COUNTER: In a small kitchen without adequate counter space a hinged tabletop or shelf that folds
flat against the wall when not in use makes a good substitute for a counter.

scorch when hot pans from the range are set directly on it. A
butcher block, as an inset in a counter, is perfect for cutting
and paring. Or consider simply setting a cutting board into the
counter surface where you will be doing most of your food
preparation. Finish it with oil for easy maintenance (use a 50–50
mixture of boiled linseed oil and turpentine, wiped on and wiped
off immediately). Cut recesses in the board, if possible, to hold
containers for seasonings and provide an area for refuse. Such
"wells" add interest as well as efficiency to a kitchen. A pastry
board for home baking and a heatproof tile or stainless-steel
section near the range are useful. Finish the surface back of your
counters with a curved molding to avoid dirt traps.

Your counter can provide more than a surface. One of the
newest materials is Pyroceram, a high-strength glass-ceramic

PLAN YOUR KITCHEN SO YOU WILL HAVE:

These surfaces	Below your elbow	When you
Counters	3 inches	serve food, stack dishes, make sandwiches
Counter or pull-out boards	6 to 7 inches	mix batter by hand, beat with an electric portable mixer, chop nuts or vegetables
Rim of the sink	2 to 3 inches	wash dishes
Cooking surface of range	3 to 7 inches	stir soups, puddings, turn meat
Fully opened oven door	1 to 7 inches	turn food in the broiler, lift heavy roasts

material made into a counter that contains cooking elements. It's a smooth, perfectly flat counter surface with four cooking areas that function best with flat-bottomed ceramic pans.

Kitchen counters can be bought in precut sections or cut to order for your kitchen. They should fit together perfectly so that there are no dirt-collecting cracks. Why not add easy-clean surfaces for all kitchen work?

In planning counter heights, consider your own size. The most comfortable work level is about 3 inches below your elbow height. Keep a sturdy, attractive stepladder on hand for safely reaching high places—and store the things you will need least often at the highest reach. Pair other items in storage—vinegar close to the oil, for example; seasonings on a well-lit shelf within easy reach of your cooking and mixing centers.

The following table shows the most frequently used types of work surfaces and their characteristics:

Types of surface material available	Features	Limitations
Laminated plastic (Formica, Micarta, Textolite, Nevamar, etc.)	Medium-priced. Available in many colors and patterns. Moisture, stain, heat and abrasion resistant. Durable. Easy to clean.	Moderately expensive. Cannot stand very hot object directly off of stove. Mars if used as a cutting surface.
Hardwood	Durable. Can be refinished to remove cuts, scorch marks and most stains. Best in sections, for cutting purposes, near sink and range. Leave unfinished or oil for simple care. Moderate price.	Subject to scratches, stains and heat rings unless properly finished. Laminated hardwood is heat resistant below 382° F. Requires some work to maintain and renew finish on surface; discolors with use.
Marble	Smooth, even, hard, heatproof, durable surface. Easily cleaned; waterproof. Moisture, stain and scratch resistant if properly used. Attractive, with some choice in color. No upkeep cost.	No resiliency; noisy and hard on dishes. Not acidproof. Fats and oils may affect color. High initial cost. Heavy weight requires sturdy support and increases freight cost.

Types of surface material available	Features	Limitations
Stainless steel	Handsome in appearance. Easy to clean and maintain. Durable. Heatproof, moisture proof, recommended next to range or sink center where heat and wear are factors.	Expensive. Not quiet or resilient. Scratches show on some types (satin finish does not show fine scratches). Cannot be used as cutting surface.
Vinyl sheet plastic	Resistant to stain, moisture, abrasion and heat below 275° F. Moderately priced. Easy to install. A quiet work surface. Available in many colors and patterns.	Not as durable as some other surfaces.
Linoleum	Attractive. Available in many colors and patterns. Inexpensive.	Surface scratches if used for cutting. Not as long-wearing as many other surfaces.
Ceramic tile	Many design effects possible. Heatproof, waterproof, stain resistant. Durable.	Relatively expensive Not resilient or quiet. Hard to keep the grout (between tiles) clean.

Planning is as planning does

The best-laid plans for kitchen centers and appliance placement can be disorganized by a careless, thoughtless user. If you open the refrigerator door for eggs, turn to the work counter, remember the forgotten milk, go back to the refrigerator, then back to the counter, decide to add cheese, and repeat the performance—you're not thinking! Before you begin, plan all the motions needed for the task at hand, whether you're preparing a snack, a meal, or cooking ahead for a special occasion. Then complete as much of each task as you can at each center. Save as much time as you can on cleanup by such simple devices as peeling onto a square of paper towel, wiping up spills as they occur, cleaning pans as you go along—quickly and easily, with nonstick finishes. Figure out how many motions you can save by dovetailing tasks—even learn to do two things at once!

Choices for extra efficiency

Plan to accommodate some of your family's special interests when you design a kitchen. If you want a kitchen that is also a sitting room, with flexibility of seating and activities, plan to install as much equipment as possible in "island" areas and in mobile carts that can be shifted about the kitchen at will. If you enjoy cooking for a gallery of onlookers, a center island lets you bring the top burners out into the room so that you can join in the conversation as you cook.

Whither the laundry?

In planning kitchen equipment, you may also want to consider laundry washing machine and dryer placement. While these are most efficiently set near water lines, it is debatable whether they are best placed near the kitchen or near the bedroom, where more laundry is collected. The truth is, in forward-looking home and apartment unit planning, the laundry appliances are being installed in or near the family bathroom rather than in the kitchen. Which serves your needs best?

Colors and coverings

Choose the kitchen colors that you will enjoy seeing every day, but consider the following points:

It is important to have a complete color scheme in mind before you begin. If you are uncertain about effective color selection,

---

CLEANING HINT: To remove stains from an enameled sink, put down a layer of paper towels, then pour in household bleach until the towels are soaked. Leave them for a half hour or so, then remove the towels and scrub the sink with cleansing powder.

you will find it easy to consult color experts for help in your planning. Check your phone directory for interior decorators. Visit several at their offices, to find out whose taste appeals to you; or check with the local branch of the American Institute of Designers, or with department stores or kitchen planners. Interior decorators may work solely on the fee received as a percentage of your purchase or on a fixed-fee arrangement.

Begin by selecting the colors of your long-term investments—the appliances, the cabinets, and counter tops. Since these will probably not be replaced in years, their colors must be basic to your overall color scheme. Then select the floor covering, for luxury of comfort underfoot, now available in kitchen carpeting or resilient floor coverings, as well as for color. Generally, it is best to paint the ceiling a shade lighter than the walls, for a sense of spaciousness. Washable acoustical tile is now available for kitchen ceilings, and the kitchen is a good place to start cutting down the noise in a home.

Plan colors to function for you—sunny hues in a dark room, cool ones where a room might seem too warm. Lighten cleanup chores with a spatter-patterned floor covering. Consider using color to highlight patterns of movement in the kitchen, as a subtle guide of beauty. Use bright colors for flash identity of storage units, and enjoy the fun along with the function. And remember that space-expanding white is still the best bet for making a small kitchen seem larger. A washable paint, particularly hard-surfaced enamel, is eminently practical.

The more modern the materials you choose for your walls, floors, and ceilings, the fewer kitchen cleaning problems you'll have. This age of plastics has produced a wide variety of gleaming new wall coverings. Plastic tiles or panels are available in a variety of sizes and colors that freshen a worn-out kitchen. Their mirror-smooth surfaces can be wiped clean with a damp cloth or washed with soap and water. Where metal channels are required at corners and at joints between panels, they add a bright trim to the wall. You do not have to contend with chips, cracks, or peeling when you install plastic coverings, and they don't stain or fade.

Surfaced with baked enamel, steel and aluminum tiles are fire-resistant and provide a permanent and functional wall covering that is attractive to the eye. Ceramic tile and structural glass are worth your consideration. They can be more expensive, but they make a highly serviceable wall.

Linoleum, particularly inlaid, continues to be a popular wall product. It can be installed with rounded, dirt-free corners.

Wallpapers and fabrics are satisfactory for kitchen use if plastic coated to resist water, oil, and grease stains. Whether you choose a textured or glossy finish, paper so treated is really washable and easy to maintain, if you do not use scouring powders on it. Self-sticking, adhesive-backed plastic wall coverings simplify do-it-yourself renovations, particularly in small or especially worn areas, such as back of ranges and counters where food might splash or splatter. They also enable you to carry out a mix-match decorative scheme by covering small boxes and storage areas or equipment doors to match counters or walls. Put a strip of molding at the top edge to make wood-grain plastic covering look extraordinarily like a panel of wood.

Color cues:

- Avoid using equal quantities of several colors. One main color should be used in about two-thirds of the kitchen area, concentrating on large, unbroken spaces.
- Try to have some areas plain, some patterned, but limit patterns to only one or two areas.
- Use color to change apparent size. White, especially, and light colors make a room look larger. Dark colors make a room look smaller.

KITCHEN-REFINISHING TIP: Save any leftover paint or wallpaper to refinish canisters and accessories to get a perfect match in color or design.

- Cool colors (blues and greens) make a room look larger; deep shades of warm colors (red, oranges, and yellows) make it seem smaller.
- Either match colors exactly or don't use colors that are so much alike that they look as if they were supposed to have matched and didn't.
- Painting a ceiling lighter than the walls will make it appear higher; if darker than the walls, lower.
- For a spacious effect, blend your kitchen colors with those in adjoining areas.
- An easy way to coordinate a color scheme is to use the primary color in one room as the accent color in another.
- Neutral colors allow the greatest flexibility in the use of accent colors. Bright colors contribute individuality and warmth.
- The room will look larger if the woodwork is painted the same color as the walls.
- Patterned work surfaces show dirt less than solid colors.

Wall coverings	Advantages	Limitations
Paint	Easy to apply yourself. (Select color carefully. Large areas of a color appear much darker than sample color.) Use a plastic-based enamel for kitchen washability.	Less durable than other types of covering.
Ceramic tile	Wide choice in color and design.	Relatively expensive
Glass tile	Attractive in appearance. Permanent, easy to maintain.	Very expensive.
Wallpaper	Washable types available. Easy to apply. Wide variety of patterns and colors available. Variable price range.	Least durable wall covering.
Wall linoleum	Attractive. Easy to apply. Long-lasting. Washable.	Moderately expensive.

Style underfoot

Floor covering is one of the major considerations in your kitchen color scheme. Personal likes and dislikes are important factors in your choice of color and pattern. Ease of maintenance, durability, and cost vary widely; almost any color you can think of is available. A variety of effects can be achieved through imaginative use of color and pattern. A narrow kitchen can be made to look wider, adjacent living areas can be made to blend with the kitchen floor covering, and work areas can be defined. Large patterns with strong color contrasts are suitable for large kitchens. In very tiny kitchens, only relatively small-scale patterns should be installed, or one single decorative element inlaid in the center of the floor. Diagonal lines running across the floor will visually widen it; this type of pattern is a good choice for a narrow room. Gently curving diagonal lines bring welcome relief to a rigidly rectangular kitchen. Setting alternate stripes of bright and subdued colors at an angle has the effect of pushing out all four walls. Custom floor designs of this sort can be achieved for very little additional cost by combining several patterns.

Since ease of maintenance is often the deciding factor in the selection of a floor covering, keep clearly in mind that a neutral or medium color with at least some pattern is easiest to keep clean and fresh-looking. Although a floor covering should be washable and resistant to soil and staining, it should also have some resiliency for walking comfort and for minimizing noise.

Here is a list of the most popular and satisfactory kitchen floor covering materials, and their good and bad characteristics:

Type of Floor Covering	Good Features	Limitations
Nylon kitchen carpeting	Integral rubber backing increases its resiliency for walking comfort. Noiseless. Spills wipe up easily. Surprisingly inexpensive, luxurious, and long wearing.	Not quite so resistant as other floor coverings to grease and certain spilled foods, but damaged places can be replaced easily by inlaying a new section of carpet.

Type of Floor Covering	Good Features	Limitations
Vinyl-asbestos tile	Relatively low in cost, $2-3 a yard. Durable. Easy to maintain. Resistant to grease, oil, and alkalies.	Not so resistant to indentation as solid vinyl. Somewhat less sound-absorbent than vinyl.
Solid vinyl tile	Highly resistant to grease and alkalies. Very durable.	Fairly expensive, $7-16 a yard.
Vinyl sheet flooring	Medium in price, $3-10 a yard. Resists wear, grease, and alkalies. Very easy to maintain.	Only fairly durable.
Linoleum	Moderately priced, $3-6 a yard. Easy to maintain.	Only fairly durable. Little resistance to alkali stains. Less durable usually than vinyl sheet.
Asphalt tile	Suitable for use over cement. Low in cost. Alkali resistant. Fairly easy to maintain.	Only fairly resilient. Not so "quiet" as other types. Hard to maintain unless heavily waxed.
Rubber tile	Very quiet. Resilient. Excellent durability.	Not so resistant to grease, oil, and alkalies as some of the other materials. Expensive.
Vinyl-covered cork tile	Resilient. Easy-to-maintain clear plastic over true cork.	Very expensive. Not so resistant as other types to grease, oil, and solvents.
Ceramic tile	Beautiful and long-lasting.	Hard underfoot, and difficult to clean. Expensive.

Kitchen lighting

Unfortunately, lighting often gets only the most casual treatment in the planning of a new kitchen. Good bright light makes food preparation and cleanup easier—and safer, too, because it helps prevent accidents. Warm, friendly, pleasant light can make the kitchen an inviting place. Harsh, cold light fights this idea.

Incandescent bulbs or fluorescent lights come in warm whites and pinks that are flattering as well as easy on the eyes.

Lighting for the kitchen falls into two categories, general and local. General lighting should provide bright, diffused overall lighting for the kitchen. Local lighting over a work area such as a sink, a range, or a countertop should provide a high level of concentrated light for each specific task—cleaning vegetables, chopping or slicing, reading recipes, scouring pots and pans.

With a little imagination, more efficient general lighting can take the place of the standard ceiling fixture. Since today's kitchens usually have work areas dispersed along the walls, leaving the center free, it seems only reasonable to move the general lighting away from the center of the room. Recessed fixtures can be installed over work centers. Four incandescent fixtures used near the corners of a medium-size kitchen give good light for work and also produce an interesting pattern on the ceiling. Obviously, light sources mounted near to wall-hung cabinets make it easier to select things inside the cabinet when the doors are open.

Lighting for each work area should be provided by a fixture or fixtures mounted above the work surface and set to avoid glare. Light must fall on the area in front of the person at the work area to prevent working in one's own shadow. Light-colored work counters and walls reduce brightness contrast; matte or semimatte finishes diffuse light best. Highly polished surfaces may create an uncomfortable glare, but are always easier to clean and high gloss is an "in" look today. Dark colors absorb light and need extra illumination.

The greatest variety of seeing tasks, and the most difficult, are performed at the sink area. The light here should be focused ahead of the worker and should be widespread and diffuse enough to eliminate harsh shadows. A 36-inch-long flourescent light or three 60-watt incandescent bulbs are recommended.

Local lighting must also be adequate at the cooking area. A range hood with one 100-watt or two 60-watt bulbs hidden under the front edge of the hood do an adequate job. If there is no hood over the range unit, and it is located against a wall or under high cabinets, a fluorescent wall bracket is recommended. It should be at least 36 inches long (30 watts).

Consider installing a local light source for every work surface that is 3 feet long or longer. Fluorescent lamps are generally used because of their linear shape, cooler temperature, and higher light output.

With a kitchen planned for happy as well as functional food preparation, it pays to put the work-in-hand into clear focus.

Cool it!

Air pollution is one aspect of modern living you can control in your own home. In the old days the family would gather in the kitchen in the winter to keep warm near the range, and sit out on the back porch in the summer to keep cool. Although today many families live in controlled temperature environments, the problem of controlling the environment in the kitchen is somewhat more complex than elsewhere in the house.

When food is being prepared, the area near the range may become uncomfortably warm. To keep the kitchen both cleaner and cooler, efficient ventilating systems remove heat, smoke, odors, grease, and moisture. Such a system is particularly important in an open-plan kitchen. If possible, an exhaust fan installed in the wall somewhat away from the range will remove moisture-laden air, cooking odors, and gases—particularly oils and fats escaping into the air in gaseous form. Keep your distance though—an exhaust fan too close to the burners can pull the heat right out from under the pots.

Even more efficacious and becoming more popular is the range hood with a ducted fan that exhausts these by-products to the outdoors. These serve more than the dictates of comfort. Cooking fats in the form of hot gases turn back into solids wherever they come in contact with cold surfaces. A house without a ducted fan in the kitchen (or a ductless hood) has to be redecorated more frequently. Fat in gaseous form, when it strikes the cold wall, solidifies back into fat combined with the dust it picks up in its gaseous state. Water in vapor form rises from steaming pots on the range and acts in even more harmful ways if it is not ducted to the outside, working its way into the woodwork and sheathing of the house, especially in cold weather, and leading to hidden conditions of rot and mold.

Under conditions in which a hole in the kitchen wall to the outside is an impossibility for one reason or another, ductless hoods with absorption filters can be mounted on wall or cabinet above the range, their efficiency depending on the size of their filters—and the householders' care in keeping them clean. Follow your manufacturer's directions carefully on this.

But a ventilating fan that really removes laden kitchen air to the outdoors is always preferable, even if the only available opening is a window. An exhaust fan permanently installed at the top of a double-hung sash should have a cover or a set of louvered blades that blow open when the fan is turned on and close automatically when it is turned off.

Any electric fan should perform its functions indefinitely if you simply keep it clean and oil it—a drop or two once a year.

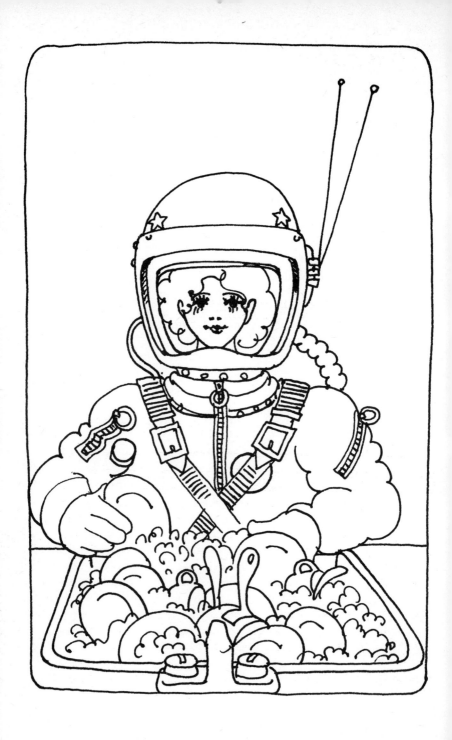

Chapter 2

How to equip a modern kitchen

Today's homemaker in the kitchen, working with a broad range of equipment, is using it less for meal preparation "from scratch" and more for heating prepared foods and putting gourmet touches on them. Still, for important occasions the full complement of kitchen equipment gets turned on for the production of dazzling meals in the sheer enjoyment of the art of cooking.

What turns a chore into a creative cooking coup? The space to store the foods you need in cupboards, refrigerator, and freezer, handy when you want them; small appliances—beater, grinder, chopper, blender—to serve as a battery of ready assistants; cooking equipment to meet your every need, from an open grill to a burner-with-a-brain, its temperature control built in. An ardent baker will want two ovens. If you enjoy such niceties as warm plates, a warming attachment for the range, or a warming cycle in the dishwasher, may be in order. If your family likes crisp roasts, a rotisserie is in your picture. Teenagers in the family will press for an ice-cream-making attachment in the refrigerator. A man who enjoys cooking may crave a butcher block. Whatever you invest in kitchen appliances to add pleasure to your meal preparation will pay off in happier meals and in a sense of achievement for the cook.

With all the equipment choices available, the big revolution in kitchen planning may be only in its early stages. Designers may soon discard the traditional concepts of a kitchen and plan it not as a room but as a series of coordinated functional centers, located where they are most wanted and where they are most useful. Equipment will become:

- Not a refrigerator and freezer, but a series of small cold units with individual temperature and humidity controls. These might appear in the kitchen for raw-food storage, in the living room and recreation room for cold drinks and snacks, in the kitchen for late drinks.
- Not a cooking range or oven unit or even top units, but various applications of heat by conduction, infrabroiling, and even microwave oscillation, all available at either surfaces or niches, closed or open.
- Not a dishwasher, but an electronic cleaning unit to sterilize and clean dishes and pans and whisk them back into readiness.

Today the kind of equipment purchased is directly affected by the type of residence in which it will be used and the space available. People living in rented quarters where space is limited should consider double-duty small appliances, like toaster ovens, or appliances that do not require permanent installation, such as portable dishwashers. Home owners, on the other hand, should be more concerned with efficiency and be sure that the plumbing, electrical, or gas requirements for new appliances can be met, or be prepared to have proper connections installed. The actual cost of an appliance should be measured in terms of amortization over its projected period of service, matched against its value in time and effort saved.

Changes in residence often mean changes in equipment. A first home furnished with scatter rugs and cotton curtains may require different equipment from that needed to care for wall-to-wall carpeting and heavy, full-length draperies—the difference between an electric broom and a heavy-duty vacuum cleaner, for example. Equipment should be evaluated in terms of both present and future needs, taking into account the expansion of the family.

People's motivations for buying new kitchen equipment may vary from a desire for increased efficiency to a desire simply to have something new. In almost anyone's house there are pieces of equipment and gadgets that are hardly ever put to use. Some families are motivated to buy appliances but not sufficiently motivated to learn to use them. An inexpensive purchase like a cake decorator that is never used is no great loss, but an expensive appliance like an espresso machine that stands idle or is not employed to its fullest potential is a poor investment.

How best to evaluate modern kitchen equipment for your own needs? Any plan for a well-equipped kitchen begins with the range and refrigerator-freezer.

Innovations in ranges

The old-fashioned coal stove used to be the center of kitchen activity, a place where the family gathered to taste Mother's recipes and to keep hands and feet warm. Major changes have taken place in the kitchen since the time of the coal stove. Today there are slide-in ranges that can be set between cabinets, built-in ranges, and eye-level ranges. There is wide variety of models and styles of both gas and electric ranges. The average

---

TO CLEAN OVEN: When the oven cools off after being used, remove any greasy or burned-on food at once; Teflon-lined oven panels should be removed and washed with detergent and water. For other finishes, use one of the chemical oven cleaners that softens and loosens food; or use a soap pad with household cleanser. Keeping oven walls and bottom clean helps to eliminate excess smoking when oven is being used.

service life of a modern kitchen range is 15 years. Since it is
an appliance that you will use daily over the course of these
years, its selection should be based on fact, not fancy.

To have the range that will give you the most satisfaction,
you should decide which basic type you prefer. Both gas and
electric ranges offer efficiency of control. Gas is cheaper in
some areas; electricity in others. Check your local utilities' rates
and your utilities' home economics service for comparative costs
of operation.

Making the choice between a gas and an electric range is
largely a matter of personal preference. If you are replacing a
range, it may be best to continue with the same kind of fuel,
because installation cost may be a factor.

Actual cooking speed with gas is about the same as with
electricity today. Some women find that the infinite heat adjust-
ment on gas burners offers more flexible temperature control,
but others find that the five to seven fixed-heat settings on
electric units are entirely satisfactory, especially if two of the
burners have varied-heat levels. In addition, some electric ranges
are now equipped with infinite controls, and some gas ranges
have definite settings on the burners. Both may have thermostatically controlled burners or units to control surface cooking
temperatures, automatically timed ovens, meat thermometers,
and other special features.

In actual practice, some women find gas more responsive and
prefer it for top burners. On the other hand, electric burners
can be readily adjusted, if used with skill, and are safer to
leave over a period of time. While some cooks argue vehemently
for one or the other, the most enlightened have *both* available—
gas burners for egg cookery and sautéeing, electric ones for such
uses as slow braising and long simmering. Electric ovens are
satisfactory for most baking, and safer in use; gas is sometimes
preferred for browning and broiling. Both gas and electric
ranges are available in five general types:

- *Free-standing range.* One-piece unit with surface units
  (burners), oven, and broiler. This is compact and economical, but not flexible, except in choice of models.

- *Built-in range.* Generally separate surface units and ovens. Designed to fit special kitchen arrangements, it cannot be moved readily and may be more costly than free-standing models unless you are remodeling or designing a completely new kitchen. Built-in top burners are available in two-, three-, and four-burner units. Some have a griddle, a rotisserie, or a gas fired grill in the center of the unit.
- *Slide-in or drop-in range.* A complete unit designed to be set between cabinets and to look as if it had been built in. Some models have side panels available so that they may be converted at a later date to free-standing ranges. These have great advantages in flexibility of placement, and with increased use, manufacturers may offer more models and sizes.
- *Eye-level, bi-level, or high oven range.* Consists of top burners at countertop height and oven(s) and broiler(s) above the cooking top. Some models, designed to be mounted on base cabinets or specially constructed units, are referred to as "eye-level consoles." These offer visibility, but require extra space.
- *Stack-on unit.* Self-contained, completely finished exterior, designed to be mounted on a counter-top base cabinet or specially constructed unit. Its eye-level oven is located adjacent to, rather than above, the top burners. This takes away some counter space; the loss may be replaced with a movable counter or island.

Forward design thinking in ranges tends toward the use of separate heat modules located in relation to efficient traffic patterns for food preparation and serving.

Once you decide which type you prefer, your next consideration, when selecting a range, is the cooking capacity you need. This depends on the size of your family and the amount of surface cooking, baking, and broiling you do. Surface units (burners) on ranges are available in groups of two to six in various arrangements and sizes. Separate surface units can be installed flush with the top of your counter.

Ovens in free-standing ranges (still the most common) are

single or double, and such ovens vary in size. They may be located below the cooking surface to the left or right, or across the full width of the range. Eye-level ovens also are available on ranges. Separate ovens may be inserted into the wall or installed on top of a counter wherever suitable space is available. Broiler units can be located in the top of the oven or in a separate compartment, or even installed close to your serving area. A rotisserie offers a new range of easy delicious meals.

You may wish to consider the practicality of having two ovens in your kitchen arrangement. A second oven is a delight when you want to bake a cake at the same time you are roasting meat, but it is superfluous unless you bake, have a large family, or entertain a great deal. You may want to consider having one oven below a cooking top and one above it. Ovens installed above a cooking top are generally not so deep as conventional ovens but are often wider to provide the desired capacity. Where there is an additional oven below the cooking top, the upper one may be smaller because it is intended for use as an auxiliary oven, ideal for such niceties as warming bread or plates.

Whether or not you decide to have two ovens, it is important to have your main oven installed at the most convenient working level. How can you decide the height that will be most suitable? Research at the Home Economics Department at Cornell University found that separate ovens should be placed so that the top edge of the fully opened down-swinging oven door is between 1 and 7 inches below the user's elbow height. The reason for this is that the convenience of a separate oven depends on how easily the housewife can lift food in and out of the oven, turn over broiling food, and inspect it. (The standard, generally, is to have the open door at the same height as the counter top.)

If the opened oven door is a few inches lower than your elbow, you will probably find that you can use your arm and shoulder muscles to best advantage in lifting things in and out of the oven. Most people can handle heavy things such as hams, turkeys, or large roasts with less strain if they can place them in the oven at, or slightly below, their elbow height or carrying level. When the oven is placed low enough for comfort in lifting and turning food, you may not be able to stand erect directly in front of the oven and see all of its contents. The simple way to avoid bending is either to pull out the oven rack with the food on it, or just step back for a look.

In general it is better to place your oven so that you do not have to lift too high. Safety is important, too. When the top of the opened oven door is below your elbow, rather than above, there is less risk of burning your forearm on the edge of the door as you reach in or out of the oven. A heat-resistant counter beside your oven makes it easier to use. You can put hot food down, as soon as you take it out, and close the oven door immediately.

Another important consideration when selecting a range is the construction of the unit. Look for construction features that provide:

- Removable Teflon-coated oven liners for easy cleanability in ovens.
- Outside finish of acid-resistant porcelain or baked enamel, chrome, or stainless steel.
- Top and back splash panel in one piece with rounded corners, for easy cleaning, and recessed range top to prevent spilled foods from running down the sides of the range.
- Handles and switches of heat-resistant material or insulated so they won't get hot.
- Convenient controls, easy to read and adjust and positioned so that you never have to reach across a burner.
- Well-fitting oven door with a lock stop; oven vent to carry off heat and fumes located so that the wall behind the oven does not become discolored; four to five open-shelf supports for varying position of racks; sturdy rust-resistant oven racks with lock stops to prevent pan tipping; and adequate insulation for safety and to retain heat.
- Broiler with easy-to-clean pan; a removable porcelain enamel, aluminum, or chromium-plated steel rack in the pan and narrow slits or holes in the rack to drain drippings

from heat and reduce smoking; and supports at several positions to adjust the distance of the broiler pan from the flame. Self-cleaning features pyrolitic (through high heat) or catalytic, through chemical additive to porcelain.

If you invest in a more expensive range, you will find one or more thermostatically controlled burners. These have a sensing disk mounted on a spring to push the disk upward and provide close contact between the sensing element and the utensil. The disk regulates the amount of heat required to maintain selected temperatures. The temperature settings may range from approximately 130°F. to 400°F. Satisfactory results from the use of thermostatically controlled burners or units relate to the suitability of the utensils used on them. The pan selected should have a flat bottom that makes firm contact with the sensing device; the pan's bottom should cover the heating unit or burner.

Cleaning is made easier today with design features such

as Teflon linings, removable doors, and pull-out interiors. For easy cleaning of the burners and range tops, wipe up spills immediately with paper towels or a soft dry cloth. The same applies to the broiler; remove the pan from the compartment as soon as broiling is finished, and sprinkle it with liquid detergent to loosen grease. After the pan has cooled, wash it in hot soapy water.

A recent development in kitchen equipment is the oven that cleans itself automatically. It is available in both gas and electric ranges. Chemical decomposition of matter by heat is used in the process; high temperature causes oxidation of food soils. The extra cost of this feature appears to be worth the labor saving, but a vented hood or kitchen exhaust fan is necessary for disposing of the heat involved.

A reminder: It is wise to provide for ventilation at the oven area to keep the kitchen cleaner and cooler. A range hood with a fan and duct to the outdoors will exhaust the by-products of cooking at the source and keep kitchen walls (and the range itself) cleaner. A ductless hood with an absorption filter of activated charcoal will remove smoke, grease, and odors, but not heat and moisture.

Another innovation is the cooking counter, a glass surface over four burners. It functions best with flat-bottomed pans.

Refrigerators and freezers

Not so many years ago fresh food was stored in an icebox to prevent the growth of bacteria. But iceboxes were poorly insulated, and this necessitated shopping every day.

Today the modern refrigerator and freezer allow (and encourage) the housewife to shop less frequently with the assurance of proper food storage. Because there are more freezers, more foods on the market today are packed to require storage at below-freezing temperatures, which makes the selection of the unit all-important.

There are two types of refrigerators, the conventional refrigerator now becoming rare and the combination refrigerator-freezer. The frozen-food compartment of the conventional refrigerator is enclosed inside the top or bottom of the unit behind a lightweight inner door. Such a compartment maintains a temperature of approximately 15°F., which is suitable for freezing ice cubes and for short-term storage of frozen foods. But 15°F. is too warm for rapid freezing of foods or for storing frozen foods for long periods of time. A conventional refrigerator may be your best buy if you already have a separate freezer, or if you shop frequently and have little need for long-term storage of frozen foods, or if you can fit the price into your budget more easily than the price of a combination refrigerator-freezer.

The combination refrigerator-freezer provides space for the refrigeration and storage of fresh foods, for freezing fresh or cooked foods, and for long-term storage of frozen foods. Combination models usually have two outer doors, one for the freezer and one for the refrigerator. Each compartment is separately insulated and has separate cooling coils. Temperatures in a true freezer should be maintained at 5° to 0°F. or below; frozen foods may be stored here for weeks and months. The freezer compartment may be either at the top or bottom of the refrigerator. Having the more frequently used refrigerator door above, at the handier level, and the freezer below seems a more efficient arrangement than the other way around. There are now models that have a full-height freezer and refrigerator side by side, with separate long narrow doors in the same unit.

A combination unit may be your best buy if you have no food freezer, if you have need to store frozen foods longer than one or two weeks, or if you can afford the higher price and slightly higher operating cost of a combination model.

Before purchasing either a conventional refrigerator or a combination unit you should determine the storage capacity you need, depending on the size of your family, the amount and type of food you plan to store, and your shopping habits. Fresh-food storage compartments should provide approximately 8 cubic feet for a family of two, and 1 cubic foot for each additional family member, plus 2 cubic feet for entertainment needs. The freezer space should provide approximately 2 cubic feet per family member. Next check the space you have available for the unit itself. Both free-standing and built-in models are available to fit just about every space requirement. Check also whether a right- or left-hand door opening is best for the location you have in mind. If a refrigerator and freezer are placed side by side, have one on the left side open to the left, the other to the right.

A separate freezer

The decision to buy a separate freezer is one that needs careful attention. Such a purchase is as important for convenience as for saving money. If you acquire one:

- Use frozen foods that need only defrosting (and heating) and no additional preparation before serving.
- Buy foods in quantity to reduce the frequency of your shopping trips.
- Prepare foods in quantity, and wrap and freeze some for reheating when needed. This is most frequently done with dishes that take lengthy preparation, such as spaghetti sauces, casseroles and stews, cakes, breads and pies (see Chapter 3). Yet even a broiled steak tastes fresh-broiled if defrosted and heated quickly just a few minutes in a frying pan. Frozen marinated meats are particularly tender and delicious.
- Take advantage of special sales and seasonal values to buy in quantity.

This selection of the type of freezer depends largely on personal preference and the amount of space available. An upright model requires less floor space than a chest freezer. A chest type of freezer requires more clearance to open the door, which swings upward—and, of course, more floor space. In general, upright models are more expensive than the chest types, however.

Away with defrosting!

A refrigerator performs most efficiently when there is little or no frost coating; defrosting should take place before more than a quarter of an inch of frost has had a chance to accumulate. For refrigerators that must be defrosted manually, the control should be set at "off" or "defrost." Frozen foods in the freezer compartment should be removed to the refrigerator space. Ice-cube trays can be filled with warm water and placed in the freezer space to hasten defrosting. As soon as the compartment is free of frost, all surfaces should be wiped dry and the temperature control reset. Frozen foods can then be replaced in the freezing compartment and the rest of the refrigerator cleaned. A solution of baking soda in water can be used for the interior of the refrigerator. Several models of electric defrosters are sold that help to speed up manual defrosting and eliminate the use of pans of hot water. Never use an ice pick or any other sharp instrument to loosen the ice. You can puncture the unit very easily.

Automatic and push-button defrosting are available on many models of refrigerators. Automatic defrosting is accomplished in several ways; the refrigerating cycle is interrupted long enough for any accumulated frost to melt (a heating element may accelerate the melting). Frost melts and runs out through a pipe into a drain pan where it evaporates by heat from the condenser or by the action of a special heating element. Defrosting may occur periodically every 24 hours if initiated by a timer that is on only when the compressor is working or when the door has been opened a predetermined number of times.

Push-buttom defrosting allows the user to select his own time for defrosting, since he initiates the process. It should not be confused with the so-called "frost-free" refrigerator-freezer, in which frost does form and can be seen but is melted automatically.

Automatic defrosting is available in most top-line freezers. For units without this feature, a plastic scraper can be used to scrape the frost off shelves and walls. Complete defrosting should be necessary only once or twice a year. Follow suggestions in the freezer instruction book.

An automatic icemaker in a refrigerator or freezer is an investment in convenience and time saving, and is one kitchen appliance that may be particularly appreciated by the man of

FREEZING HINT: If you need a lot of ice cubes for a party, empty the trays several times and store cubes in plastic bags in the freezer.

the house. In addition to the cost of the unit itself, it is necessary to budget for a water-line extension that provides a flow to the cube maker. The cost of this will vary with location and house plan, but $40-$50 seems an adequate estimate. The advantages are:

- A constant supply of ice cubes, ready when you open the door
- Saving of effort in tussling with ice-cube trays
- No spills or wipe-ups
- Extra production of cubes to store in plastic bags in the freezer for such peak use as parties

If you calculate that a man uses five frustrating minutes every evening getting out a cube tray, emptying it, refilling it, and replacing it, that's 30 hours a year of wasted time. At $4.00 per hour, this would be worth $120, or more than twice the cost of a $50 unit.

Auxiliary small refrigerators and freezers at little over $100, located in eating, recreation, and work areas of the house, may be worthwhile investments in convenience. The refrigerator loaded with cold drinks, cubes, pickup food, ice cream, and sherbet enables you to have snack foods available when and where they are wanted.

An automatic ice-cream-making attachment for your freezer is an example of equipment that may offer values beyond the monetary investment. Even though you can buy ice cream for less than the cost of making it at home with heavy cream, you can hardly calculate the value to your family of freshly made, home-flavored ice cream, "frosted" desserts, low-calorie "ice milk," and frozen fruit-juice "slush," available whenever the desire arises.

Dishwashers

A dishwasher may well rate as a homemaker's most universally desired appliance. It can end most of the drudgery involved in cleaning up after meals if it is used properly. Dishwashers also make it possible to use hotter water, stronger detergents, and high drying temperatures for more thorough cleaning and elimination of bacteria. Small families often store soiled dishes and pans in the machine until they have a full load, rather than wash them after every meal (assuming they have a good supply of dishes).

Dishwasher capacity depends on the type and size of dishes used. The manufacturers have begun work on the establishment of realistic capacity standards.

Not everything should be washed in a dishwasher. China with a gold or silver trim or overglaze decoration can be damaged in a dishwasher. Cooking utensils with burned-on food will not wash clean without some pretreatment, unless they are Teflon-coated pans. Large utensils that take up a lot of room may be more easily washed by hand. Be sure to follow instructions of the cookware manufacturer regarding dishwashers. Plastic, rubber, and wooden items should not be washed in a dishwasher.

Satisfaction with a dishwasher depends on proper use. The housewife who doesn't bother to scrape off the leftover food on her dishes may face the fact that most dishwashers cannot yet dispose of refuse—although this is coming. Hardness of the water, improper loading, and insufficiently hot water may also account for poor cleaning.

Loading methods vary somewhat with type and location of

EQUIPMENT HINT: If you are considering the purchase of a dishwasher, a plate-warming cycle is a great convenience. It permits you to warm dishes quickly with no danger of breakage.

the washing mechanism and the design of the dish racks, but a good rule of thumb is to place all dishes so that water can reach all surfaces. Some dishwashers have racks that require systematic loading, while others have more open racks to allow random placement of dishes. The former encourages correct loading, but the latter allows for more flexibility in accommodating items of miscellaneous size and shape. Dishes also must be placed so that they dry properly. Place all pieces so that water will drain away from them and not accumulate in the concave bottoms of dishes.

Dishwashers may be purchased either as portable or permanently installed appliances. Portable models are usually top-loading, and permanent installations are usually front-loading, which leaves free counter space on top. For front-loading machines, loading is easiest when upper and lower racks slide out independently of one another. Some portable models are adaptable to permanent installation, a good solution for the apartment dweller who hopes to buy a home.

Disposers

A food-waste disposer is designed to destroy most fruit rinds and vegetable parings, fats and greases, coffee grinds, small bones, and other food waste. It is not designed to destroy paper, metal, foil, glass, cloth, string, large bones, or highly fibrous materials such as artichokes. The grinding unit is electrically driven and is installed directly below the opening of the sink. Although a disposer can add greatly to the housewife's ease in getting rid of garbage, special codes in some areas prohibit its use, while other areas require its installation in a new house. In most communities, however, the decision is left up to the homeowner, but plumbing codes often have specific requirements for installation, and you should check on them before purchase. For instance, when a disposal unit is connected to the same drain as an automatic dishwasher, a backflow preventer is often required so that if the drain becomes clogged, the sewage will not back up into the dishwasher.

To use a food disposer, you scrape food waste into an opening in the bottom of the sink, being careful not to let silverware and other small metal objects fall in by mistake, risking damage to both objects and disposer. To operate, the user turns on both the cold water faucet and the motor switch. Continuous-feed models allow the user to add food waste while the unit is in operation. The typical disposer has a dual-purpose top which, when in place, will let water in but prevent the waste from flying out. The motor is usually turned on by a wall switch. Batch-feed models operate only when a switch top is inserted and locked in position (safest for use in a home where there are children).

Small appliances

In the field of electric housewares, new equipment and gadgets intended to make the housewife's work easier appear almost daily. Since many small appliances perform multiple functions, the housewife might well consider which functions are most appropriate to her own needs.

Among the appliances with combined functions now on the market are toaster-broilers, cooker-fryers, and waffle baker-grills. Sometimes a simple attachment may add multiple functions to an appliance motor. For example, food blenders and mixers now come with attachments for coffee grinding, ice crushing, juicing, and knife sharpening. Also available now are special units in which one motor, sometimes recessed in a counter or wall, provides power for several food-preparation attachments, including beater, blender, grinder, sharpener, and juicer. While these offer efficiency of single-motor use, it is wise to check the efficiency of the individual components in operation.

Let's examine more closely the appliances available for food preparation.

Mixers are used for stirring, creaming, and beating. The mixer's electric energy that replaces your own labor usually results in a better product. How frequently a mixer is used seems to depend on its accessibility. Your decision in choosing between a hand-held model and a table-stand model may depend on where you will be able to store the appliance. What are the types of task you want the unit to perform? Hand-held portable units sometimes have three speeds and less power than the table-stand models, which usually have eight to twelve speeds.

Portable models sometimes come with such attachments as a drink mixer, a whipper, a knife sharpener; table-stand models often have several attachments available, but a power adapter may be necessary. Beaters are easily cleaned on both models, but the power head should never be immersed in water. Rather, wipe it clean with a damp cloth after each use.

Blenders use small powerful blades to chop, puree, or liquefy fruits and vegetables, chop nuts, combine the ingredients of sauces, dips, soups, and drinks, and speed food preparation in many ways. Blenders do not substitute for mixers, since they cannot whip cream or egg whites, nor mix complete cake batters, nor mash potatoes satisfactorily. But used to capacity, a blender more than earns its keep. Some blenders even beat while they blend—a boon for sauce-making. Blenders now come with detachable cutter blades that greatly simplify cleaning. Safety tips: *Unplug the unit before cleaning.* Blades inside the mixing container can be cleaned by filling the container with warm water, adding a drop or two of detergent, and operating the unit to make suds. Rinse the same way, and dry by running it a moment after rinsing.

Drink mixers have less power than blenders and perform with a beating rather than a cutting action.

Although most of the electrical housewares used for cooking are portable, they require more storage space than their non-electrical counterparts. The controlled-heat cooking that can be done with these appliances makes food preparation easier. They also make it possible to move cooking out of the kitchen to anyplace where there is sufficient electrical power. If the appliance is one that heats foods, it is important to look for well-designed and well-insulated handles and feet so that the user can grasp them easily without burning himself.

When the thermostatic control on an appliance is a part of the unit, the appliance cannot be immersed in water. If the control is enclosed in the handle, the unit can be immersed in water up to an indicator on the handle. Some appliances have detachable probes, a separate unit containing thermostat, control knob, signal light, and heat-sensing rod or probe mounted on the end of an electric cord. This type of control may be used to operate a whole "family" of housewares, but keep in mind that only one utensil can be operated at a time and that the control cannot be used interchangeably with other manufacturers' appliances. Removable heat probes do help to make the units easier to clean.

Coffee makers are wonderful convenience appliances. A coffee maker that does not control brewing time and then keep the coffee warm for serving, however, is of little advantage over a nonelectric unit.

Coffee makers can be either percolator or vacuum type; each has certain advantages in performance and cleaning. Of course, clean utensils are essential to good coffee in any type of coffee maker.

Electric toasters usually have wells that toast two or more slices of bread on both sides at once. Many toasters have controls that allow the user to select a range of brownness from light to dark. If a toaster has a removable or hinged crumb tray, cleaning is simplified and should be done frequently to prevent clogging the pop-up mechanism.

Toaster-ovens accommodate sliced bread or rolls or loaves on a horizontal rack. A metal insert provides a base for baking rolls or heating frozen foods. Meat cannot be cooked in a toaster-oven, but it will bake potatoes. Tip: Boil a potato in its skin for 12 to 15 minutes, then bake it (in the toaster-oven). It will be ready in about half an hour, and you'll never guess it was previously boiled!

Electric frypans are perhaps the most adaptable appliances the housewife can own. The normal unit is 10 or 12 inches square and made of stamped or cast aluminum. Features such an extra pan depth, steam vents, and domed covers increase the capacity and usefulness of such units. Units with detachable heat controls are easiest to clean. Many electric frypans now have handles on both sides of the pan, making them more attractive for table use. Many now come with Teflon nonstick surfaces, which make cleaning and maintenance far easier.

EQUIPMENT HINT: To keep the kitchen cool on hot days, use the electric skillet, not the oven, for cooking a small roast or a casserole dish. Save clean-up time with a Teflon-lined skillet.

Saucepans, dutch ovens, and cooker-fryers are all available now as electric appliances operated with probe control units. Featuring controlled heat within the unit, they take up no more storage space than a nonelectrical unit. Pouring from some units is difficult.

Rotisserie-roasters provide additional cooking capacity and flexibility and save the trouble of heating a large oven. The rectangular-shaped ovens with glass-front windows provide for broiling, roasting, grilling, and baking, or a combination of these uses, within a smaller unit than an oven. Not so heavily insulated as the oven of a range, some parts of the appliance may become very hot, and units should be placed out of the reach of children. A rotisserie is sometimes very difficult to clean. This is a handy auxiliary unit when only one oven is available.

Rotisseries and grills offer popular direct-heat cooking of food prepared flavorfully, close to the serving area. Open rotisserie models also offer entertainment value as diners watch their dinners brown, turning on a spit raised over a heating element in the base. The outside of the meat or poultry or fish becomes crisp and brown, wonderfully aromatic. High-intensity elements and open cooking result in a minimum of smoke and cleanup while assuring maximum flavor.

Electric warming trays keep cooked foods warm in the kitchen or at the table.

A waffle baker and grill combination is worth investigating because of the versatility of such an appliance. Usually two sets of grids are provided with different sides for different uses. Most waffle bakers are square; the grids are of cast aluminum. Many units now come with Teflon coatings on the grids for nonstick cooking and ease of cleaning.

Although the number of kinds of small appliances has almost doubled in recent years, care should be taken when purchasing such items to avoid duplication of function. No appliance is worth the investment if it is used only rarely and if its function can be performed as conveniently by a nonelectrical unit. It is also important to be sure that every appliance and every electric cord is labeled "UL Approved." This means it has been declared safe by Underwriters Laboratories.

Also worth noting in your investigation of small appliances is the availability of nonstick cooking surfaces on many of these units. Such surfaces are so easy to clean that they make cooking easier and cleanup swifter. They also simplify preparing nonfat foods—a great asset to the diet-conscious.

Whatever appliance you decide to purchase, always read the operating instructions on the unit itself and in the instruction book. Always be sure the control is at "off" before plugging the cord (if it is removable) into the unit.

Another new development is the appliance panel, which makes it possible to use from four to six appliances at one time without overloading the electric circuit. The panel employs circuit breakers rather than fuses. A panel may be installed flush to the wall, mounted on or underneath kitchen cabinets, or may come as part of an appliance cabinet that provides storage and work space.

Large or small, most pieces of electrical equipment come with a manufacturer's registration number and guarantee. You owe it to yourself to fill this out as promptly as possible and return it, to assure fulfillment of the guarantee.

The pots and pans in your life

There are a number of important factors to be considered when selecting kitchen utensils. They include the size of your family, the kind and amount of food prepared, methods of cooking, amount and type of entertaining, storage space available, and the importance of such items to the family. Concerning this last point, many modern kitchens are designed with exposed food-preparation centers, which call for utensils to be decorative as well as serviceable.

A wise selection of utensils does not necessarily mean purchasing a complete set, because sizes, designs, and materials offer special advantages for certain uses. Consider the number of times each specific piece in a set might be used. Only a few unused pieces eliminate savings made in buying a set.

In the selection of pans for cooking, keep in mind the time-and-motion efficiency of utensils that can go from range to table (frying pans and casserole dishes of tempered glass, oven-proof ceramic, stainless steel, porcelain-enamelled aluminum and cast iron); platters that can be used as warmers; and grill pans that can serve as platters. If you own a freezer and plan to freeze casseroles for reheating, check on the cold-heat resiliency of casseroles that can go from range to freezer to table with style as well as efficiency. You take extra pleasure in using them because of the time and effort they save, and enjoy the triple benefits in lessened preparation time, easier serving, and reduced cleanup time.

The purchase of kitchen utensils should not be taken lightly. In aggregate, their cost is often sizable, but the items should remain in use for years. The cost of utensils is usually related to the material from which they are made, with lighter-weight, less expensive materials used for inexpensive lines and heavier gauges, more expensive materials, and more distinctive styling generally incorporated in the more costly utensils.

It would be difficult, perhaps impossible, to compile a list of kitchen utensils that would be complete for the needs and habits of every family. The following paragraphs are offered more in the nature of guidelines for the purchase of kitchen utensils than as a listing of necessary items.

Saucepans and frying pans: Heat is transferred mainly by conduction for top-of-the-range cooking. It is important that heat be transferred quickly and evenly so that the part of the pan directly over the heat will not get so hot that the food scorches.

Aluminum is an excellent heat conductor, and is used both alone and in combination with other materials for saucepans and frypans. Iron is slow to heat; but once heated, it conducts evenly. Stainless steel is easy to clean and offers an attractive finish that blends well with other kitchen colors. Many man-ufacturers have added copper or aluminum to the bottoms of stainless-steel pans to improve conductivity.

Top-of-the-range cooking utensils should have flat bottoms large enough to cover the burners. Straight sides use the range's heat more efficiently than flared sides. The sides of the pan should meet the bottom in a smooth curve, without a separating seam, to facilitate stirring and cleaning. Here again, the benefits of nonstick surfaces are evident; they make both cooking and cleaning easier. Edges of saucepans (saucepots or kettles) should be rimless for maximum ease of cooking and cleaning (or they may be turned and rolled to form a flat rim or beaded edge). Rimless pans also facilitate pouring; sometimes a pan will have one lip or a lip on both sides for pouring.

Saucepans are used for cooking with water or other liquids that help, by convection, to transfer heat to the food itself. (Frying pans are usually used without liquid, so good heat transfer is especially important.) There are, basically, three kinds of saucepan: a "saucepan" has one long handle, a "sauce-pot" has two handles opposite one another, and a "kettle" has a single continuous handle from one side to the other. All should have flat bottoms for maximum even conduction of heat. Pans that have handles with holes in them can be hung in the kitchen to save cabinet storage space and also to provide a decorative background for the stove. (Be careful to hang pots sufficiently above the stove to prevent burning yourself if you reach for a pot while cooking.)

Modern cooking methods sometimes call for the use of a minimum amount of water for cooking vegetables or rely on juices already in the food in order to retain vital nutrients. Low

EQUIPMENT TIP: Use Teflon-coated pans as dessert or salad molds when they're the approximate size needed. You'll find that with the nonstick surface, the salad or dessert can be released very easily.

temperatures should be used for so-called "waterless cooking." Such cooking requires a tight-fitting cover to prevent excess evaporation; close contact between the rim of the pan and the cover increases cooking efficiency. Covers purchased for the specific pans always fit better than those purchased separately. Pans and covers should be purchased in sets. A good handle for a cover is one that is easy to grasp without burning the fingers. A ring handle at the top of a cover is best lifted with a fork. Dome covers, while they may increase cooking efficiency because of their tight fit, also may increase storage space requirements. Turn these covers upside down in the utensil to save storage space.

Frying pans range in size from about 6 to 12 inches in diameter and are probably the most used pieces of equipment in the kitchen. Most families prefer to have at least two frying pans, one large and one small. While frying pans are most often used without covers, a frying pan with a cover is useful to have for braising or other cooking methods that require moisture. Mesh-wire covers now available also prevent spatter of cooking oil or fat, while allowing moisture dissipation.

The handle should be fastened securely to the frying pan, fit the hand well, and permit easy grasping of the utensil. A handle that is too long can tip the pan when it is only partially full, as can a handle that is not firmly attached. Make sure that a loose handle is tightened before you use it. Handles that remain cool to the touch regardless of the heat of the vessel itself are best. Handles of enameled pans are welded to the steel base, and the entire pan is then enameled, leaving no seams at the joining points. Pyroceram cookware, a type of glass that can take great extremes of temperature, has detachable handles that fit onto the lip of the pan.

Nonstick-coated cookware has replaced noncoated pots and pans in many homes. Food cooked in such utensils will not stick. Some people whose doctors recommend a low-cholesterol diet find that the nonstick characteristics of Teflon-lined cookware enable them to cook entirely fat-free dishes. The nonstick properties, as mentioned before, are a blessing at cleanup time.

EQUIPMENT TIP: If you have a pressure cooker, you can cook several vegetables together without any transfer among flavors. The pressure cooker not only requires very little time for cooking, but because so little liquid is added, natural vegetable juices are preserved.

Pressure cookers are time-savers in the kitchen. Steam is made to build up in such units to reduce cooking time. Pressure cookers are usually made of heavy-gauge material with steam-tight covers. Four- to six-quart sizes are the most popular, except for home canning, for which larger sizes are more desirable. It is important to remember that pressure cookers should never be stored with the covers sealed on.

Young homemakers are often wary of the pressure cooker, remembering harrowing tales of how the lid blew off Aunt Sue's utensil and ruined her kitchen ceiling forever. But a pressure cooker is very easy to learn to use and is safe and efficient if properly used. Proper reading and understanding of the operating instructions is your best guide. The pressure must always be completely down before the cover is removed; placing the pan in cold water at the end of cooking reduces the pressure quickly. Almost any food can be cooked in the pressure cooker except those that tend to expand, foam, or thicken, such as applesauce, cranberries, rice, or split peas. These foods may foam and clog the vent that regulates pressure.

Pans for oven baking can be of slightly lighter weight than those used on the top of the range. The reason for this is that they are not subjected to direct heat and are used less frequently. However, it pays to invest in sturdy pans such as aluminum, stainless steel, cast iron, ceramic, or ovenproof glass, in standard sizes for effective recipe use. Pans should be sturdy so that they will not warp or bend out of shape with use— after all, who wants a trapezoid cake? A level-bottomed pan makes for even baking. One-piece seamless construction is highly desirable, because it facilitates cleaning. Pans used in the

SUGGESTED BASIC BAKING PANS FOR A SMALL FAMILY

2 layer-cake pans	8 or 9 x 1-½ inches deep
1 square cake pan	8 x 8 x 2 or 9 x 9 x 1-¾ inches
2 cookie sheets	15-½ x 12 inches
6 custard cups	5- or 6-ounce
2 loaf pans	9 x 5 x 3 inches
1 muffin pan	6 to 12 individual cups
1 oblong cake pan	13 x 9 x 2 inches
2 pie plates	9-inch diameter
1 tubed angel food pan	10 x 4 inches
1 shallow baking dish	1-½ quarts
2 casseroles	1-½ quarts, 3 quarts
1 shallow roasting pan with rack	15-½ x 10-½ x 2-¼ inches

oven should absorb heat quickly and evenly; dark finishes are heat absorbent, while highly polished surfaces tend to reflect radiation. When glass is used for baking cakes, it is wise to reduce the required oven temperature by 25 degrees to produce a cake similar to that baked in shiny tin or aluminum. Incidentally, too deep a pan will result in food that is not browned on top, while too shallow a pan will result in the mixture's running over the edges. Teflon-lined pans assure easy release of baked goods—an important factor in baking—as well as easy cleanup.

Cooking with style

Kitchen accessories (tools): Measuring cups and spoons should follow U.S.A. standards for best results (available from U.S. of America Standards Institute in New York). It's a good idea to keep duplicate measuring utensils at more than one center in your kitchen, since you will probably use them at each food-preparation center. Sifters and strainers, beaters, mixing bowls, forks, spoons, and spatulas should all be able to withstand vigorous everyday use without becoming bent, dented, or distorted. Teflon-coated utensils, including spatulas and spoons, are available for women who are bothered by even small scratches.

A good *rotary beater* has thin, sharp, sturdy blades; eight blades are more efficient than four.

Mixing bowls, if made of steel, aluminum, tempered glass, ceramic ware, or heat-resistant plastic can serve not only the function of mixing but also that of cooking. Glass and ceramic ware have the advantage of heavier weight, which keeps the bowl in position when the beater is in action. For ease in using, and if storage space permits, store bowls of graduated size singly rather than nested, or at least keep separate those you use most frequently.

Metal forks, ladles, mashers, spatulas, and spoons for stirring and mixing and turning have common construction features. The better quality ones are usually made of stainless steel with either integral handles of stainless steel or heat-resistant handles (made of either plastic or fine-grained hardwood). The method of joining the handle should be inspected, because if the shank is driven only a short way into the handle, it will certainly be more likely to work loose than one that goes well into or all the way through the length of the handle.

The tines of forks should be sharp, rigid, and smooth. Spatulas should be rigid near the handle but flexible enough at the farthest extension to slip under a cake or pie. Spatulas are now available with nonstick coatings.

Knives of good quality are perhaps the most essential item in any kitchen. Without proper blades, the homemaker is simply not equipped to prepare or serve even the most elementary meal. Iron and carbon are the basic materials of most knives, but other additives to the alloy plus the heat-treating process determine the quality of the blade. If not enough carbon is present, a blade darkens and stains and must be more frequently sharpened because the steel is softer. Some manufacturers add two other ingredients: vanadium, which strengthens the carbon steel, adds durability and helps hold a keen edge; and chromium, which produces a stainless steel that resists rusting and stains.

There are several methods used by manufacturers in sharpening blades, all of which are used to produce different edges with slightly different uses. The least expensive method is the flat grind without curvature. Sometimes called the "V" or taper grind, this type of edge wears quickly and requires frequent re-setting and sharpening. A roll grind is obtained by placing the lower part of the blade between two sharpening wheels that are rotating toward the blade. A hollow-ground edge is made by sharpening both sides of the cutting edge in a long, oval curve.

Most meal preparation calls for considerable cutting, slicing, peeling, chopping, coring, boning, or trimming before the food reaches the table. If the work is to be done swiftly and efficiently, it is important to use the proper knife for the job The following list identifies 18 special knives and their individual uses. This merely lists types of knives available. Many knives perform similar functions and can be used interchangeably.

- *Butcher knife* for cutting, separating, and cubing uncooked meats, fish, poultry
- *Steak knife* for slicing steaks, carving turkey and chicken, small roasts
- *Sandwich knife* with scalloped edge, for preparation of sandwich meats, cutting hard rolls, garnishes
- *Tomato knife* for tomatoes, cucumbers, carrot curls, onions
- *Utility knife* for vegetables, meats (both raw and cooked)
- *Grapefruit knife* to separate segments of grapefruit and oranges
- *Paring knife* for paring, peeling, slicing fruits and vegetables
- *Utility knife* for cutting, slicing fruits, vegetables, pies, small meats
- *Boning knife* with curved blade, for dissecting raw chicken, deboning roasts and baked hams
- *Seven-inch roast slicer,* for cutting, separating, and cubing meats, fish, poultry
- *Nine-inch roast slicer* for cutting and slicing raw roasts, cheese, melons
- *Steak and poultry slicer* for carving all kinds of fowl and small roasts, and cutting steaks

- *French chef's knife* for dicing and chopping vegetables, sectioning corn on the cob, squash
- *Two-tine fork* for assisting in carving and serving; pairs with knife to make carving set
- *Sharpening steel* to restore a blade's keenness by resetting the edge
- *Kitchen shears* for cutting poultry, fish, dried fruits
- *Cleaver* to cut through meat bones, joints; split fish
- *Kitchen saw* to cut through meat bones, frozen foods

Keep in mind that wooden-handled knives should not be placed in the dishwasher. If dishwashing is done by hand, knives with special-finish wood handles should not be allowed to soak in water. Soaking will soon ruin the finish and dry out the wood.

Knives should be stored separately to preserve the fine edges, and should be kept close to the major point of use for kitchen efficiency. Wall magnet bars effectively hold knives in readiness.

Try to use a knife only for its particular purpose; never cut bones, string, metal, or paper with knives. By using a wooden board when you cut, you will protect your cutlery, yourself, and your countertops. When cleaning knives, which should be done immediately after use, never soak them in water or detergent, as this may ruin the steel. Wash and dry knives promptly after each use.

Electric knives bring cutting energy and power to the hand of the carver. They make a functional gift, resulting in effortless, even slicing, though they are hardly essential.

Chapter 3
How to shop a supermarket

Food shopping techniques change as dramatically and as rapidly as kitchen equipment and design. Are you making the most of these changes? Yesterday's daily shopping routine has given way to once-a-week shopping. New processing techniques keep foods longer—efficient refrigerators and freezers make longer home storage practical. Homemakers can buy more economically, in larger units, and draw from the stock of home supplies as needed. Values and convenience as well as variety have soared beyond the most imaginative predictions of a generation ago.

Still greater changes are coming. The next time you push a cart through the crowded aisles of a supermarket, consider this: Technologically, we could even now sit at home at a TV telephone and view the selection at a supermarket. The equipment exists for computer ordering of what we want. A card, notched for a family unit, could be inserted in a "charge it" slot attached to the picture phone. Groceries would be delivered, precleaned, and ready to store in appropriate cold centers and food-distribution spots around the house, ready for use.

As your cart is jostled in the crowded aisle, all this may seem like the projection of a dream. Technology is in advance of the actuality; but as the changes achieved in the second quarter of the 1900's have been as dramatic as any period in history, the changes just ahead are almost unbelievable.

The great American shopping bag

How much food do you think our 200 million Americans consume in one year? Picture a freight train stretching all the way from New York to San Francisco. Add seven more alongside and load them all with food. If this staggers your mind, think of it in terms of money—some $100,400,000,000 for our national annual food expenditures—and the figure is still climbing.

An American family of four consumes an average of two and a half tons of food a year. Break this down into food groups and the estimates are: meat, fish, poultry, 1,000 pounds; dairy products, 1,000 pounds; fruits and vegetables, more than 1,000 pounds; all other foods, including breads and cereals, 1,600 pounds. All this you carry home from the market a bag at a time!

Food is big business, and it's the consumer who determines how much stock will move from shelves, freezers, and meat counters. It is consumer response that determines manufacturers' decisions on products themselves, as well as the sizes, shapes, weights, and even the designs on the labels and packages.

While economists note that the proportion of American disposable income spent for food has decreased, housewives are aware that it becomes increasingly easy to spend more for food. The American supermarket is a new kind of wonderland crowded with thousands of choice products in a challenging array. All the old economical favorites are still there alongside new gourmet, international, prepared, precooked, ready-to-serve specialties.

Half a billion meals a year

With some 45 million family units in America, the average family size is over 3½ members, almost half of whom are teen-

SHOPPING TIP: Try to do your supermarket shopping early in the day when stock is fully replenished. There are occasions, however, when perishable produce has been overstocked and can be bought at bargain prices just before Saturday closing.

agers. Moreover, many of our homemakers are teen-agers. The median age for marriages is about 18, and more children are born to mothers under 20 than to any other age group.

The mealtime statistics based on these figures are staggering. Multiplying family units by the number of members and meals per day, American housewives plan, buy, prepare, and serve almost a half billion individual meals a year. If America's homemakers could manage to save 20 percent—in time and effort as well as in money—the total savings would represent a tremendous increase in family enjoyment.

Faced with the challenge to use to advantage the plenty about them, many shoppers enter a supermarket in a kind of daze that leaves them incapable of the simplest mathematical comparisons. When the consumer steps through the door of the supermarket, she is somewhat like the young sheik who had just inherited his father's harem. As he appeared at the door he hesitated: "It isn't that I don't know what to do, I just don't know where to begin," he said.

In a study made in the mid-1960's by Colonial Stores, an Atlanta supermarket chain, and Progressive Grocer, a trade magazine, the typical shopper was analyzed. She was a 45-year-old homemaker with two children. The family owned a car and had an income of $5,850.

At about three o'clock on Friday afternoon she would hop into the car (half the time bringing the children) and drive two miles to the supermarket, passing another market on the way. She felt that prices at most supermarkets and for many competitive products were about the same. She valued especially the service, meat, produce, and merchandise variety in that order.

She generally saw the weekly food ads, but only rarely bought the advertised specials. In her typical shopping tour of 26 minutes, half her time was spent in the perishables departments—meat, produce, bakery, dairy, and frozen foods. Her remaining time was taken up in the grocery department and at the checkout counter.

The typical consumer in the study bought some of her groceries in one or two other stores, but did the bulk of her shopping in her favorite store. She generally didn't arrive with a shopping list (70 percent of those shoppers checked did not have one). She used the supermarket itself as a "reminder" of what she needed as she walked the aisles, and once she became accustomed to shopping at certain areas of the market, she was likely to stop at these areas regularly.

What, no shopping list?

You get more out of this wonderland, saving as much as 20 percent of every dollar you spend, if you come prepared with a "road map" of what's available, a clear idea of your needs, and sound knowledge of foods and how to select them. Yet, the typical shopper, according to a supermarket study, carries no written shopping list, visits the market 2.7 times a week, takes 26.1 minutes to shop, and spends an average of $7.21 per visit, allowing a mere fraction of a second to make the decision to buy or not to buy a produce. Fewer than one-third of shoppers check newspaper ads in advance; most make purchasing decisions right in the store. Yet, even in quick shopping you can easily save on your food bill by following 12 simple points:

Take stock. Note your home supplies in cupboards, drawers, refrigerator, and freezer before you set out to replenish them. Smart shoppers shop from a list.

Adsmanship. Read the ads before you shop and on the way into the market. Make the most of the savings offered.

Size. Compare costs per ounce and per serving of package contents before you buy. If packages are available in fractional sizes, simplify comparison shopping by reducing each of the nearest whole number. The best per-portion buy is generally the largest size you can conveniently store and use up before it spoils.

Type. Buy a quality and type that suits the specific use you plan for it. For instance, buy flaked tuna for a sandwich spread and solid-pack tuna to center a Salad Niçoise.

Brand. Compare costs of different brands that suit your needs, keeping in mind your family's special preferences for certain brands. The bargain that doesn't get eaten is no saving at all!

Understanding. Don't pay more unless you get better eating or more nutritional value. When Grade A brown eggs are cheaper than Grade A white eggs, buy the equally nutritious brown. Discover the savings in use of nonfat milk solids and less expensive cuts of meat.

Prepackaging. Because of economics effected by the producer, bulk prepacked vegetables and fruits are lower in price than when loose. Fancy packages hand-wrapped at the market cost more, but offer speed in shopping.

Convenience. You often pay extra for more fully prepared foods. Balance the time-saving against the extra money. Sometimes the time saved is worth the difference, and sometimes the total cost is actually less than it would be if you prepared the food yourself from scratch.

Meat. Remember that meat accounts for about 25 percent of your total food expenditure. Less expensive cuts of meat are just as nutritious as the most expensive, and in some cases (organ meats, for instance) more nutritious. The most desirable cuts bring premium prices because the demand is greater than the limited supply.

Cost per serving. When you figure the cost of anything you buy, figure its per-portion cost. For instance, 2 pounds of veal cutlet at $1.79 per pound will make 8 servings. A 3-pound sirloin steak at $1.19 per pound has fat and bone waste and will make only 6 servings. The total cost of each is the same, but the veal is obviously a better buy.

Produce. You spend almost as much of your money on fruits and vegetables as you do on meat, so it's important to buy wisely in this area. Depending on the season, fresh produce can be cheaper or more expensive than frozen or canned. Buy ac-

cordingly, selecting for a balance of flavors, textures, and food
values.

Savvy. As you shop, check the shelves carefully for special
values of interest. Supermarkets advertise leading products at
low cost to attract customers; take advantage of these real
savings. But buy only those you can really use.

Calculating women

Because so many factors other than price per ounce enter into
the decision to buy, a shopper has to learn to make complex
calculations quickly. For example, if you are planning dessert,
an inexpensive unflavored gelatin available at about 5¢ will
set a pint of liquid. The price of that liquid is up to you and can
be anything from sweetened water or juice or broth to champagne! Or, you may want to buy, as the majority of shoppers do,
gelatin combined with sugar and color and fruit flavoring; the
price is about double that of unflavored, uncolored, unsweetened
gelatin. Or if your time is very limited, and you haven't thought
to prepare gelatin in advance, you can pick up a ready-to-serve
molded gelatin dessert from the refrigerator case of the supermarket at about four times the cost of the dry powder you mix
yourself. It is ready when you want it, appealing to children
and adults alike, and still a less expensive dessert than one you
would buy if eating out. And now there are gelatin desserts in
jars and in cans to offer still more convenience at prices competitive with the refrigerated product.

Which is the best choice? Any of them might be, depending
on your time and needs at any given moment. The challenge in
shopping is to take advantage of all the variety available to meet
all your food serving needs, matching those needs against your
budget for food.

Your decision to buy

In the comparison shopping game more than price alone goes into
the evaluation of a product, of course. First there are basic
values: A large economy-size version of popped, flavored noth-

SAVINGS BY COMPARISON SHOPPING*

	Mrs. X	Mrs. Y	How Mrs. Y saved money
2 qts. milk	$0.54	$0.48	gallon vs. 1 qt.
1 doz. grade A eggs	.57	.43	medium vs. extra large
½ lb. American cheese	.43	.16	2 lb. loaf vs. ½ lb.
½ lb. cottage cheese	.20	.11	2 lb. carton vs. ½ lb.
1 lb. butter	.94	.73	brick vs. whipped
1 lb. margarine	.47	.18	brand
1 qt. tomato juice	.33	.17	1 qt. 14 oz., vs. 1 qt.
1 qt. apple juice	.27	.25	1 qt., 8 oz. vs. 1 qt.
1 lb. loaf white bread	.37	.22	brand and style
1 doz. dinner rolls	.35	.25	brand
4 oz. instant coffee	.75	.54	10 oz. vs. 4 oz.
24 tea bags	.36	.25	pkg. 100 vs. 24
2 lbs. flour	.31	.17	5 lbs. vs. 2 lbs.
3 lbs. chicken	1.29	1.20	whole vs. quartered
2 lbs. steak	2.44	1.50	chuck vs. sirloin
3 lbs. round roast beef	3.63	3.27	bottom vs. top
½ ham	3.58	2.79	shank vs. butt
2 servings lamb chops	2.08	1.20	shoulder chops vs. loin
5 lbs. potatoes	.59	.39	bag vs. loose
3 lbs. onions	.39	.35	bag vs. loose
10 oranges	.69	.65	bag vs. loose
1 lb. tomatoes	.65	.39	ctn. vs. loose hothouse
1 lb. detergent	.28	.18	5 lbs., 4 oz. vs. 1 lb., 4 oz.
toothpaste, large	.89	.49	brand
100 aspirin	1.17	.29	brand
8 oz. breakfast cereal	.33	.20	ind. serv. vs. lg. pack
1 lb. marmalade	.39	.15	2 lbs.; brand
1 can tuna	.48	.27	flakes vs. solid pack
8 oz. peanut butter	.40	.23	24 oz. vs. 8 oz.
6 oz. potato chips	.39	.27	12 oz. vs. 6 oz.
2 pkgs. frozen peas	.78	.33	butter sauce vs. plain
2 cans frozen orange juice	.50	.36	brand
1 bottle catsup	.29	.25	20 oz. vs. 14 oz.
1 pt. mayonnaise	.41	.22	1 qt. and brand
1 jar mustard	.23	.17	brand
1 bottle steak sauce	.37	.17	brand
1 can peaches	.39	.32	brand
1 can tomatoes	.33	.15	type and brand
	$28.86	$19.63	

Total saving = $9.23

* 1967 prices, N.Y.C.

ingness may be a good buy but of less intrinsic value to you than a small package of nuts that offers good food value along with a satisfying snack.

In making her split-second decision to buy or not to buy, the supermarket shopper deals with a complex series of relationships —juggling time, family tastes, cost of the item, and the subtleties of nutrition, flavor, and pure emotional satisfaction that make a product the right match for individual needs.

With all these other factors to juggle, how in the world do you decide between package A and package B of similar products? How do you decide what size offers the best buy for you? How do you decide where to shop?

The supermarket, with its large and varied selection, usually offers the best all-around buys. You can frequently save more by spending more time in one store checking values and prices than by comparison shopping from store to store, unless you

have the time and want to stock up on large quantities of pre-pared staple items.

Shopping is like any other skill—training pays. Make yourself an expert shopper by adopting the following habits:

- Prepare a shopping list as a guide, but check it out in the store, making substitutions when you find lower-priced items of equal nutritional value and satisfaction that suit your needs. If you add items to your cart, think how they will fit into your meal plans and buy accessory foods accordingly.
- Check the price of each item in terms of weight of number of servings before you buy. Don't be confused by minor fractional differences in package size. Round these out to the nearest whole number and compare accordingly.
- Keep comparative food values in mind in comparing prices. Chicken may substitute for meat; frozen or canned peas for fresh; canned applesauce for fruit cocktail.
- Buy what you can use or store efficiently in as large a quantity as possible for best value. But the large economy can of fruit juice is no buy if you do not finish it, and a large package of detergent may be a burdensome storage problem in a small apartment.
- Shop in an orderly sequence. It's practical to go down the grocery aisles first and select staples and boxed, canned, and jarred purchases. Then shop for baked goods, dairy products, frozen foods, meats, and produce, keeping delicate fruits and vegetables at the top of your cart. When you unload at the checkout counter, place these last on the automatic loading belt (if the arrangement is a manually pulled rack, place them first to avoid crush-ing by the heavier items). Your purchases are then ready for packing with staples underneath and perishables on top. Ask the clerk to pack all frozen products and re-frigerated perishables on top in double bags so that they will not defrost on the way home.

Of course, the market of the future may make all this obsolete. Meanwhile, a group of ingenious devices have been worked out to help simplify price comparisons. Some shoppers carry an automatic counter with them and keep a running tally of costs. Others use special comparison-shopping disk calculators that indicate the cost per ounce based on weight and price. In making your final decision, you can control your total expenditure and realize considerable savings by careful shopping.

Dovetailing tools and food

Take full advantage of your equipment and appliances, pots and pans, and storage areas in planning food purchases. A freezer is most economical if it is used to capacity. Easy-clean nonstick-lined casseroles are especially advantageous if you keep them filled with prepared foods ready to take out of the freezer, heat, and serve. Your closest and storage areas function best if you inventory and rotate stocks of foods and supplies for economical meal preparation. Buy when you can get the best prices—use at your moment of greatest advantage.

Scheduled bargains

It pays to set a regular day, every week or every other week, for major food purchasing. Many small, hurried trips to the market are less economical, obviously wasteful of effort—and add up to higher expenditures. Try to make your trip on the day when store specials go into effect and at an hour when the store is least likely to be crowded. Supermarkets have buying and storage peaks too. These specials of theirs offer you a real chance to save on your food dollar.

Reading the label

The one accurate source of information about the product you are going to buy is the label. It pays to read it—for price, description of product, yield in portions, and general use. Every label is subject to careful inspection and designed to help you decide whether a product will meet your needs. It often includes suggestions for use. Make the most of these to get the best value from your purchases. In each instance, choose the quality you need to suit your purpose and taste.

Choosing prepared foods

Labels are particularly important for foods that have been canned, frozen, dried, or otherwise prepared for use. Check the label for:

- Name of product
- Brand name of the manufacturer so that you will know what to expect next time you buy (or don't buy) its products
- Net contents to show the amount and often the servings contained
- List of ingredients in the order of their quantity. The ingredients listed first is the highest in amount by weight, followed by all others down to the smallest. This is extremely important in helping you determine that the value and nature of the product "Burgundy Sauce with Beef" is a different product from "Beef in Burgundy Sauce." If all ingredients are not listed, that product may be subject to a Federal Standard of Identity, which is your guarantee of basic quality.
- Food additions so that you know the nature of such ingredients as sweeteners, thickening agents, and color. All these must meet government standards for safety and purity before they are used, and the level of use is generally controlled.
- Style described on the label. For example, you may want tomatoes whole, diced, sliced, in sauce, puree, paste, or a combination of these.
- Variety of product—such as slender, straight Blue Lake green beans or broader, curved varieties. Check style of pack: plain, in sauce, sweet, tart, or in a combination pack.

Check canned foods before buying for:

- Informative labels, as described above
- Containers that are firm and have no leaks or bulging areas (beware of botulism in bulged cans—dangerous)
- Style of food that best suits your needs at the most economical price
- Can size that provides the number of servings most convenient and economical for you

COMMERCIAL CAN SIZES

Size	Weight	Approximate amount
6-ounce	6 fluid ounces	¾ cup
8-ounce	8 fluid ounces	1 cup
No. 1 (Picnic)	10-½ ounces	1-¼ cups
No. 300	1 pound	1-¾ cups
No. 303 (or 1-½)	1 pound	2 cups
No. 2	20 ounces	2-½ cups
No. 2-½	29 ounces	3-½ cups
No. 3	33 ounces	4 cups
46-ounce	1 quart; 14 fluid ounces	5-¾ cups
No. 10	106 ounces	12 to 13 cups

Check frozen foods before buying:

- Freezer cabinets should be clean and free from excess frost. Cabinets should be filled only up to the freezer line (about 6 inches below top of cabinet). Temperature should be indicated and must be 0°F. or below.
- Choose packages that are frozen hard, free of sticky residue, and without external frost. Heavy cracky frost or ice crystals in the package indicate that the temperature has fluctuated en route or in the cabinet, which could result in deterioration of quality or flavor.
- Buy only the quantity of frozen foods you can store properly until used (see table in Chapter 4 for freezer storage time). Pack frozen foods in insulated bags, or group a number of frozen packages together in double bags; take home and store promptly in the freezer.

- Even if you do not have a freezer, you can take advantage of certain frozen products, particularly juice concentrates, vegetables, and fruits. Store them as you would fresh products.

Meal determination

Meal planning and marketing have a chicken-and-the-egg relationship. Whether one precedes the other is a matter of debate, but there is no doubt of the interrelationship. The quality of the meals at home depends on what is brought home from market.

The basic foods needed each day are the same at every income level. Whatever the expenditure of time, at least some money and effort is involved in food preparation. Eat something every day from each of these four food groups to meet your daily nutritional needs:

- Milk, cheese, 2 to 4 servings; sometimes ice cream
- Meat, fish, poultry, 2 or more servings; eggs, 3 or 4 per week
- Fruits and vegetables, 4 servings (including 1 citrus fruit or other food course of vitamin C, and 1 green leafy vegetable)
- Breads and cereals, 4 servings

Before you leave the supermarket, check to see that you have bought proper proportions of each of the basic food groups to meet your family's nutritional needs. The best "buys" in the world won't be worth buying if they don't provide what you need for well-being.

By the same token, the most nutritional foods in the world won't be good buys if your family doesn't enjoy them. The nutritionist's beloved kale, treasure trove of vitamin A, does no good if it is left on Junior's plate. Family likes and dislikes must enter into your choices as much as price and value.

You can, however, influence those likes and dislikes by your methods of preparation. That same kale cooked, chopped (or whirled in a blender), and creamed or baked with mashed potatoes into a puffy souffle or pancake takes on new character

and appeal—and your budget profits from economical and
nutritionally significant food choice. What's more, having learned
to accept the flavor in this form, Junior may come to like kale
in its unadorned form.

The types of meal to be served will influence food choices too.
Are there school-aged refrigerator raiders who need between-
meals snacks? Do you provide quick meals-in-hand that meet
their needs? An apple or a cold chicken leg is as accommodating
to schedule as a pizza wedge or a candy bar—if you have them
ready. Do you prepare a welcome nibble with nutritional value
to go along with a relaxing drink when your husband comes
home?

Stretching food dollars

Statistics for family food expenditures vary, but for most
American families food represents the largest single living ex-
pense.

Rising taxes and erosion of the value of the dollar make it
increasingly important to buy food carefully and stretch the
food-budget dollar as far as it will go.

There is a direct relationship in time available, interest in
food preparation, and the cost of meals. However, the very
lowest income segments of our society have discovered an interesting fact of life: You can't cook as cheaply at home as some
prepared foods can be manufactured. Baked beans and many
soups, for example, cost less to buy than to prepare at home.
Moreover, they deliver more nutritional value for the most than
homemade specialties.

Many other foods partially prepared outside the home offer
economies in money as well as in time. It is a luxury to squeeze
your own fresh orange juice—a delightful, refreshing, and nutritious luxury, but usually more expensive than frozen orange
juice concentrate.

Canned corn, canned asparagus, canned spaghetti, and canned
beef stew are all better buys than buying fresh ingredients to
make them, according to studies by the U.S. Department of
Agriculture. Of course the results are different, too, and it is up
to you to decide where to draw the culinary line.

Cooking to taste

Your time, interest, and skill in cooking influence what you buy. So do attitudes about foods based on your culture and background. You may discover new adventures in taste, along with economy, if you leave some old prejudices behind. Epicurean kidneys and brain often go to waste in markets or are sold for pet dinners because few Americans bother to prepare them.

Gourmet Cassoulet is a tasty blend of inexpensive white beans and bits of duck, pork, and sausage. Your own specialty may be as simple as layering bread and bacon with grated cheese,

covering it with egg-beaten milk, and baking to a tasty and
inexpensive soufflé-like meal. Or, you may discover a casserole
that transforms fish fillet into a family favorite. But if you are
not going to take the time to cook it—or not use all you
purchase—the best food economy is a poor buy.

America is said to have the best-fed garbage pails in the
world. Small wonder, when homemakers discard the livers and
gizzards of chickens, pour off the liquid in which vegetables are
cooked, and disregard many thrifty food buys because they've
never tried them.

Those same livers add up to a bonus dish when accumulated
in the freezer, then cooked and chopped. The gizzards and
vegetable liquids can contribute to homemade or prepared soups.

How to buy meats

Meat is usually the most expensive item on the menu. You can
therefore make the most dramatic savings by purchasing meats
carefully, storing them properly, and cooking to avoid waste.

Women quickly become expert at judging color, fat, and bone;
markets and butchers are judged by the way meat performs in
the pan.

Check labeling, packaging, for information. The Federal government inspects for wholesomeness all meat shipped across
state lines, to make sure that it is processed under sanitary
conditions. Some states and cities require inspection before meat
can be sold locally. Federally inspected meat is stamped with a
round "U.S. Inspected and Passed" seal.

Grading of meat is an optional service. Beef, veal, and lamb
may carry a shield-shaped stamp; pork is seldom graded because
there is less variation in tenderness. The grading classifications
for veal and lamb are similar to those for beef:

Prime: Highest grade of beef from choice steers. Since supply
is limited in comparison to total beef production, most is sold
to fine restaurants. Prime meat has the greatest amount of fat
marbling and is the most tender. ("Marbling" means that thin
threads of fat, not chunks, are spread through the meat.)

Choice: Highest grade of beef commonly sold in retail stores.

The lean is usually bright red and firm. It is well streaked with little veins of fat and has a thick creamy white fat covering. This grade is flavorsome and tender.

Good: Still of excellent quality, but more moderately priced. Meat is a slightly darker red, has less fat and marbling and somewhat thinner fat covering than Choice.

Commercial and **Utility:** Lowest grade available in retail stores. Has thin fat covering; usually used for braising or stewing.

Tender cuts of meat, the 25 percent that is most desired in the United States, come from the little used muscles along the back of the animal. Meat cuts that come from the strongly developed leg and thigh muscles are less tender and contain large amounts of connective tissue, but have the same nutritive value and can be tenderized or cooked to delectable goodness. Savory marinades also tenderize meats. Grinding meat makes it more tender. Instant meat tenderizer used before cooking brings luxury tenderness to less expensive cuts and enables you to broil and serve as sliced steak cuts of chuck that would otherwise need long, slow braising to break down the tough tissues.

Commercial grades may be used rather than Federal grades and stamped on meat by packing companies to indicate quality. Packers' brands have variable meanings. A "select" label by one packer may mean a quality of meat different from another packer's "select" brand. Companies and stores also vary to some extent on what they mean by "trimming" or how much fat and bone are removed. If you want to be sure of a particular trim, check a brand you know or ask for "butcher service" at your market.

Choose thrifty meat cuts. Take advantage of less expensive cuts of meat to make savory stews, pot roasts, and tender braised meats, or tenderize them for broiling or roasting. For dramatic results buy a thick slice of chuck or round, or even a rump roast. Slice, moisten with cold water and sprinkle with instant tenderizer. Pierce all over with sharp long fork tines, repeat on second side. Grill just until rare, let stand a few minutes, then slice into one-fourth-inch-thick slices and serve with pride. The price of the meat does not determine its food value. Lean cuts of beef, veal, pork, and lamb are similar in nutrients except that pork has more thiamine (vitamin B_1). If you want to save money, try these less expensive cuts:

Beef: For pot roasting, heel of round, rolled rump roast, English or Boston cut, chuck roast, beef shanks, and short ribs. Also stewing beef, oxtails, brisket, tongue, and ground beef are penny savers.

Pork: Economical rib or loin ends instead of center cuts are good for roasting; also try shoulder roast, shoulder steaks, pork hocks, ham shanks, and smoked picnic shoulder.

Lamb: Square-cut shoulder roast, neck slices, shanks, shoulder chops, and stew meat are least expensive. These combine well with practically all vegetables.

Veal: Ground veal is delicious in meat loaves or patties; veal shoulder roasts and shoulder steaks are good veal buys.

Liver, kidney, brains: Organ meats are great nutritional buys and frequently are of low cost. These are quick-cooking foods. Inexpensive beef or pork liver has as much nutritional value as calves liver.

Check servings per pound. When you buy meat consider the amount of meat you will get per serving. The price for a pound of beef chuck roast may be about the same as that of ground beef liver. But in most cases, a pound of bone-in roast will provide only about half as much meat as a pound of ground beef or liver. The other half of the pound is lost in bone, excess fat, and drippings. Here is a guide to servings:

- Boneless meat, whole or ground: 3 to 4 servings per pound
- Meat with bone, such as rib roasts, steaks, chops: 2 servings per pound
- Bones surrounded by small amount of meat, such as short ribs, spare ribs, and pigs knuckles: 1 serving per pound

When your favorite cuts are on special, buy two. Or buy a large cut at a lower price per pound and use it for several dishes. A large beef chuck roast can be divided into thirds; the center can be used for pot roast, and the rounded boneless end for stew. The remaining piece can be sliced lengthwise into Swiss steaks. And you have three main dishes prepared in different ways.

Read the grocery ads. Look for meat specials and plan accordingly. Over a long period this represents considerable savings. Check advertised meats for grade as well as cuts to establish value.

If you have any questions about the meat you buy, don't guess. Ask the butcher or meat manager. He will also take care of special orders, special requests on boning or cuts; but ask him in advance if possible; or stop at the meat counter first, and do the remainder of your shopping while your order is being prepared.

Many meat managers try to help the shopper by indicating on labels or display posters how the meat should be used. One cut may be labeled "oven roast" and another "pot roast," or a cut-up shoulder of lamb may be marked "lamb for stew." Sometimes recipes are included along with a special buy of the week or month.

How to buy dairy products and eggs

Next to meats, dairy products and eggs take the biggest chunk of the average family's food dollar. They also offer dramatic possibilities for savings.

Fresh milk is usually the highest in cost, but even here you can make important savings by checking the prices for large-size containers (if you can use the quantity) and store prices as compared with home delivery. Nonfat milk solids enable you to make drastic savings. If you combine nonfat milk solids (reconstituted) with fluid whole milk, you can enjoy milk with very acceptable flavor for drinking or cooking. You reduce calories and save about one-third on your milk bill.

Cream is also priced according to fat content. Heavy cream contains 36 to 40 percent fat; light cream, 18 percent fat; and the prices are in ratio. You can combine the two, let stand a day in the refrigerator, and have a whipping cream at more economical cost.

In buying eggs, compare prices of different sizes of eggs at the same grade. When there is a difference of more than 7¢ per dozen between large and medium, or medium and small eggs,

the smaller egg becomes the better buy. For most recipe
purposes, they may be interchanged. There is no nutritional
difference between white and brown eggs.

The neglected sea harvest

Fish offers an economical and delicious source of protein foods
too little used in American diets. As a result, fresh fish counters
are disappearing from supermarkets and fresh shellfish are increasingly difficult to find. However, supplies of frozen and
canned fish are available and offer many thrifty choices aside
from the ubiquitous tuna and shrimp—neither of which tastes
like other fish. Investigate your local supplies and be adventurous
about trying new types of fish—broiled, fried, or boiled. If you
cannot decide among them, buy small quantities of several
varieties of fish and prepare the fisherman's stew, Bouillabaisse,
for a new adventure in eating.

In buying, check to see that frozen fish is firm and without
crystals. Make sure fresh fish is clean and without surface slime.
Buy fish only from a refrigerated case. If you catch your own,
clean and refrigerate or freeze promptly.

How to buy poultry

Whether chicken, duck, turkey, or Rock Cornish hen, poultry
has changed dramatically both in character and supply since the
1950's. As farm products they were subject to the vagaries of
season and reproduction, but now they are virtually manufactured on poultry farms, bringing a large and consistent supply
of tender birds to the market at low prices. These are now
generally so uniformly produced that you are virtually assured
of tenderness and quality in an excellent protein food, relatively
low in calories.

Chickens themselves have been streamlined in production to
yield a high proportion of meat in young and tender birds,
turkeys developed in smaller size, ducklings manufactured in
uniform size and with less fattiness—yet this is only part of the
new poultry shopping story. New chicken products include

chickenburgers and chicken franks. Chicken parts sold as packaged legs, breasts, wings, etc., offer the choice of preparation for elegance or economy, according to your needs and budget. For example, you can buy thrifty chicken necks and backs for soup stock, legs and thighs to fry for a picnic, breasts for a party casserole.

Turkey parts, generally sold frozen, make it possible to prepare a practical, small turkey roast at any time, again with a choice of lower-cost or more expensive cuts. Specialities such as holiday goose are available frozen, more thriftily priced than the fresh products. Small Rock Cornish hens make practical party servings, or interesting individual roasts.

In buying poultry it is worthwhile to check for:

- Clean skin with few feather marks. No bruises or discoloration. Wide, plump body with fleshy breast and legs. Tip of breastbone should be soft and flexible in a young bird. Fat should be well distributed over breast and thighs, color pale and waxy.
- The U.S.D.A. inspection mark. It assures you that it has been inspected for wholesomeness. All poultry and poultry products shipped between states and provinces must carry this mark.
- Government grades on ready-to-cook poultry. These indicate quality. Brand names may indicate different quality as determined by each producer. If branded poultry is graded, it conforms to the government standards for that grade.

How to buy fresh fruits

The sooner fruit is eaten after picking, the more flavor and nutritive value it has. It's smart to buy fruit during the peak of its season and to eat it as soon as possible. Prices are lowest whenever a particular fruit is most plentiful—a factor a wise shopper should not overlook. When fruits are out of season, compare prices among canned, frozen, and dried products.

- *Don't buy only because a fruit is low-priced.* The so-called bargain may be simply overripe. Fruit deteriorates rapidly once it has reached its prime, and the waste in preparation may offset the price reduction.

- *Don't buy on size alone.* Large-sized fruits are not necessarily the best quality. Choose fruit on the basis of eating quality rather than appearance. While appearance and quality are often closely related, sometimes a fruit with a very attractive appearance may be a poor buy because of some internal characteristic such as overmaturity. On the other hand, a fruit with poor outer appearance may have excellent eating quality.

- *Don't handle fruit carelessly.* "Don't pinch the bananas" is a saying that makes economic sense. No one wants to purchase damaged fruit; the grocer's loss gets passed on to the consumer in higher prices.

- Enjoy your fruit purchases. Display nonfragile fruits in attractive arrangements until they are fully ripe or eaten. When too ripe or tender for this, store in the refrigerator.

Make the most of fresh vegetables

The fresher the vegetables when you use them, the better. Flavor and crispness, and some food value too, are lost when the vegetables are held at market or stored at home for too long. This is especially true of leafy vegetables, such as spinach and lettuce. Tuber and root-type vegetables are less perishable; therefore they may be bought in greater quantity and stored in a cool, dry place.

Green vegetables are especially important in meals because of the nutrients they contribute, particularly vitamins A and C. Both intensity of the vegetable's green color and the part of the plant from which it comes are clues to its food value—in general, the greener the vegetable the richer it is in vitamins and minerals. Dark-green leafy vegetables may carry several times as many nutrients as green fleshy pods (snap beans) or green seeds (peas or lima beans).

- *Select vegetables, as you do fresh fruits, with considera-*

tion for season and supply. Choose vegetables that are mature, well-colored, fresh-looking in appearance, and free of bruises, skin punctures, and decay.

- *Buy only what you need.* Give some thought to what vegetables will be used in the next two or three days, remembering that leafy vegetables are especially perishable.
- *Shop carefully.* Don't buy damaged vegetables even if the price is low. U.S. grades on prepackaged vegetables can be your guide to quality. Moisture-proof cellophane and other transparent plastics are effective wrappings to retard water loss during marketing.
- *Handle vegetables carefully.* Someone must pay for loss by careless handling.
- *Let vegetables such as tomatoes and avocados ripen at room temperature.* Low storage temperatures retard maturation as well as deterioration. A temperature of 60 to 70 degrees is best; but don't place them in direct sunlight.
- *Double the enjoyment of sturdy vegetables* such as squash or eggplant by arranging in centerpiece decorations, then cook as needed.
- *Choose vegetables for variety to add interest to menus.* Use vegetables for other than main course, as appetizers or salad. Artichokes make a delectable first course. They are filling, too, so that a lighter main dish may be served. Stuffed mushrooms, tomatoes with herb oil-vinegar dressing, and savory eggplant are other good first courses. Vegetables add flavor and color to soup.
- *Cook with care.* Pan-braise vegetables with a little oil and a minimum of water, covered; or steam in a perforated basket in an ordinary pan, for bright color and maximum retention of vitamins.
- *Cultivate a green thumb for extra vegetable enjoyment.* Whether you raise herbs in a windowsill pot, or have a truck garden for seasonal enjoyment of the first tender sprouts of asparagus, sun-ripened tomatoes, or incomparable fresh-picked sweet corn—you will discover that nothing you set on your table can compare with the pleasure and the quality of your own harvest!

How to get the most from grain foods

Although grains are the staff of life, we are fortunate that in this affluent country we need not lean too heavily on this staff.

Processing prepares grains for eating by removing some of the hard outer husk; this also removes some of the food value in the whole grain. New knowledge and skills replace these with comparable food values in products labeled *enriched* or *restored*. Read the labels on bread and white flour products to find whether they are enriched—particularly if your children rely heavily on sandwiches and grain products.

Breads and baked goods vary greatly according to type and degree of preparation. Sometimes you pay more for partially baked goods that you finish and serve at home, but the fresh aroma may be worth the price. If your budget is tight, check the market for day-old bread and baked goods often sold at savings—or discover the joys of baking your own bread.

Buying the fat of the land

Heavy cream with high fat content costs more than light. The most expensive grades of meat are well larded with fat, both externally and between the tissues. Some of this fat might be better left unbought, if your family is concerned about overweight or high cholesterol. In making your fat purchases remember that:

- Fats are divided into saturated (animal fats) and polyunsaturated (vegetable oils). The American Heart Association urges you to cut your intake of saturated fats and substitute a proportion of polyunsaturated fats in your cooking and salad making for the sake of your family's health. The polyunsaturated vegetable oils are corn, peanut, soybean, cottonseed, and safflower.
- Margarine costs considerably less than butter and may be used for many of the same purposes, although the flavor is not the same. You may prefer to use butter for certain spreads and delicate sauces and cut down on the total amount used.

The power of your purchases

A final note on your place in the American economy as a food purchaser: In all your food selections remember that you wield the purchasing power that spells success or failure for any product. If a product satisfies you, buy it again. If you are disappointed, exercise your pocketbook ballot.

Food	*Unit*	*Approximate Measure*
DAIRY PRODUCTS		
Butter	1 bar (¼ pound)	½ cup
	1 pound	2 cups
Cheese, American	1 pound	2 cups (4 cups grated)
Cheese, cream	3-ounce pkg.	6 tablespoons
	8-ounce pkg.	1 cup
Cheese, cottage	1 pound	2 cups
Cheese spread	5 ounces	½ cup
Cream, heavy	½ pint	1 cup (2 cups whipped)
Milk, evaporated	14½ ounces	1⅔ cups
	6-ounce can	¾ cup
Milk, nonfat dry	9⅝ ounces	3¼ cups
		(12 cups reconstituted)
Milk, sweetened, condensed	15 ounces	1⅓ cups
EGGS		
Whites, fresh	8 to 11 whites	1 cup
Yolks, fresh	12 to 14 yolks	1 cup
FATS AND OILS		
Margarine	1 pound	2 cups
Vegetable shortening	1 pound	2½ cups
Suet, chopped	1 pound	3¾ cups
FLOUR		
All-purpose	1 pound	4 cups sifted
Cake flour	1 pound	4½ cups sifted
Rye	1 pound	4½ to 5 cups
Whole wheat	1 pound	3½ cups unsifted

Food	*Unit*	*Approximate Measure*
SUGAR		
Brown	1 pound	2¼ cups firmly packed
Confectioners	1 pound	4½ cups sifted
Granulated	1 pound	2 cups
FRUITS		
Apples	1 pound	3 medium (3 cups sliced)
Bananas	1 pound	3 medium (2½ cups sliced)
Berries	1 quart	3½ cups
Candied fruit	½ pound	1½ cups, cut up
Dates, pitted	7¼-ounce pkg.	1¼ cups, cut up
Dates, whole	1 pound	2¼ cups (2 cups, pitted) (1¾ cups, cut up)
Lemon, medium	1	⅓ to ½ cup juice; 1½ to 3 teaspoons grated rind
Orange, medium	1	⅓ to ½ cup juice; 1 to 2 tablespoons grated rind
Prunes	1 pound	2⅔ cups (4 cups cooked)
Raisins	15-ounce pkg.	3 cups
MISCELLANEOUS		
Bread crumbs	1-pound loaf	10 to 11 cups fresh bread crumbs
Chocolate, unsweetened	8-ounce pkg.	8 squares, 1 ounce each
Coconut, shredded	1 pound	5 cups
Coffee, ground	1 pound	80 tablespoons
Almonds, in shell	1 pound	1 to 1¾ cups
shelled	1 pound	3½ cups
Pecans, in shell	1 pound	2¼ cups
shelled	1 pound	4 cups
Peanuts, in shell	1 pound	2¼ cups
shelled	1 pound	3 cups
Walnuts, in shell	1 pound	1⅔ cups
shelled	1 pound	4 cups

Dash	=	Less than ⅛ teaspoon
1 tablespoon	=	3 teaspoons
4 tablespoons	=	¼ cup
5⅓ tablespoons	=	⅓ cup
8 tablespoons	=	½ cup
12 tablespoons	=	¾ cup
16 tablespoons	=	1 cup
1 fluid ounce	=	2 tablespoons
2 cups	=	1 pint
2 pints	=	1 quart
4 quarts	=	1 gallon
8 quarts	=	1 peck
4 pecks	=	1 bushel
16 ounces	=	1 pound

Chapter 4

How to store foods— how to freeze

A version of Parkinson's law applies to households of every size. Possessions increase in number and size to fill the space available. Nowhere is this more true than in the kitchen. Utensils and foodstuffs seem to accumulate and fill all available shelves and drawers. It takes organization to make the most effective use of these spaces. With sound organization, you can utilize those same spaces to save food dollars and preparation time.

As family purchasing agent, you will spend an average 25 percent of the family income for food. If you were living in Great Britain it would be 40 percent; and in Russia, 60 percent. If it's any comfort, their costs are rising as inexorably as ours.

As the superintendent in charge of the family warehouse, you can capitalize on your expertise in shopping economically by buying in quantity while practical and storing with care.

For efficient warehousing, always move the old stock forward when replenishing shelves so that it is used before the new supplies are tapped. If yours is a large family or if you have youngsters reaching into your shelves, you probably will want to straighten and rearrange supplies at the time the market order is made up. This will help you determine whether you have the space to take advantage of supermarket specials. The best time to clear out the refrigerator is just before you go shopping.

From market to kitchen

When you come home from the market and unload your purchases, group them according to their storage requirements, but store the frozen foods and perishables immediately. Unload near the freezer and refrigerator so that foods requiring refrigeration can be stored quickly while the door is open.

Canned goods and staples should be stored nearest the place of first use; reserve supplies should be shelved according to type of food or supply.

Dual storage for certain staples and foods-in-use saves steps and wasted motion. Salt and pepper needed at the mixing center are also needed at the range. Flour used by the cup when baking a pie or cake should be kept in a large canister at the mixing center; it is a good idea to keep a small container of flour near the range for thickening sauces and gravies. Keep a cup measure in the flour container to serve as a scoop.

Keep staples covered in closed containers, since food spoilage is caused by dust-borne yeasts and molds as well as by bacteria. Airtight glass containers can be decorative jars of rice, various shapes of pasta, or dried peas, beans, or lentils.

According to your needs and cooking personality, herbs and

MEAL-PREPARATION HINT: Keep a shaker of mixed salt and pepper near the range for general-purpose cooking. Blend 3 parts salt and 1 part pepper.

SPICE TIP: Place your spices in alphabetical order on the spice shelf, and put them back again in the same spots when you finish using them. Easier to locate, especially if you have a great variety of them.

spice logically belong at the mixing center, at the range, near the refrigerator, or wherever the salad gets tossed. Herbs and spices lose their flavor quickly once their containers are opened; they should never be stored near the heat. Keep salt warm and dry, but keep herbs in a cool place.

Most herbs and spices should be replaced every six months or whenever they lose their freshness. This is one case where large, economy sizes may be poor buys. Whole spices, ground as you use them, stay fresh longer.

Coffee and tea, like herbs and spices, should be kept in airtight containers. Coffee, which contains volatile oils, should be stored in the refrigerator once the vacuum seal is broken on the can. Coffee beans, both before and after they are ground, keep better under refrigeration. Tea should be transferred to an airtight container. Tea is most conveniently stored near the range (or electric tea kettle) so that it may be readily added to the teapot when the water comes to a boil.

The breadbox is home for baked goods, but a breadbox takes up a lot of counter space. In warm, humid weather a small family may have trouble using up a loaf of bread before it molds. Bread not being eaten quickly, particularly whole-grain breads, should be refrigerated to retard mold. Crackers, however, need their own separate airtight storage, especially in humid weather.

Bread, interestingly enough, keeps better in the freezer than anywhere else. In the refrigerator, although mold is retarded, bread loses its fresh texture rapidly. It comes from the freezer as fresh as it went in, provided it is properly wrapped and thawed while still in its wrapping.

The sweet life

Sugars are best stored in jars or canisters near the baking and mixing center, in small containers near the range, at the table in a sugar bowl, each with appropriate measure or spoon. Syrups, honey, and molasses should be kept in their original containers on the shelf near the mixing center. Vermont's time-honored maple syrup, however, has a tendency to mold if it is kept too long under mold-favoring conditions. Refrigeration retards mold growth, but remove syrup to warm it before it hits yours waffles. Mold—known as "mother" in New England—can be skimmed off and maple syrup heated to boiling to stop further growth.

> STORAGE HINT: To keep brown sugar from lumping and becoming hard, transfer it from the package to an airtight container, and store it in the refrigerator.

Fats and oils

Fats and oils—lard, vegetable shortening, and the various cooking and salad oils—need storage according to individual characteristics. Unopened containers keep indefinitely at room temperature; opened fats and oils keep best refrigerated. Lard is more perishable than vegetable shortening, but except in very hot climates stabilized lard can keep several weeks without refrigeration after opening. The producers of fine Spanish olive oil do not recommend refrigerating their product because it impairs the oil's bouquet permanently. If the oil seems to lose freshness, they suggest warming it up, along with a piece of orange peel and a few cloves, which are then strained out. However, all but the purist will probably find the refrigerator longer-keeping and more practical.

A little experience is the best guide as to which size container can be used to advantage before contents start to go stale or

STORAGE HINT: After deep-fat frying, do not discard the oil or fat, but cool it slightly, then ladle into strainer lined with cheese cloth; cool, cover, store in refrigerator. Every so often, add fresh oil or fat.

rancid. Considerable savings can be effected by purchasing oil by the gallon and decanting to a small container for cooking and table use.

Nuts, pickles, and canned joys

Nuts, a notably oily food, have the same tendency to rancidity that pure oil has if kept too long at too warm a temperature. If someone sends you Georgia pecans or lavishes you with English walnuts, there will come a time when they must be used or put under refrigeration or frozen.

Pickles, piccalilli, hot-dog relish, catsup, and chili sauce do not need to take up room in the refrigerator unless you want to serve them chilled. Mustard, mayonnaise, and salad dressing, however, do require refrigeration once opened. If in doubt, check the label.

Olives need not be refrigerated until just before serving time. After opening, return unused olives to the canning liquid and

STORAGE TIP: Most unrefrigerated shelf foods keep best at temperatures between 50° and 65° F. But unless you have a nice, dark, cool pantry, this storage range is often difficult to maintain. Next best thing: buy foods such as uncooked cereals, prepared mixes, spices and crackers, flour and hydrogenated shortening in small enough quantities to avoid deterioration before they are used up.

STORAGE HINT: To keep crisp cookies crisp, place in a tightly covered jar. Moist, soft cookies should be placed in a separate container, not with the crisp ones. Freshen cookies that have become soft by placing them in a slow (250° F.) oven for 5 minutes.

store in the refrigerator. If a white film develops on top of the liquid, simply rinse the olives before serving.

Jams and jellies can be stored near the eating area or near the dishes in which they are served. In a small household it isn't surprising to see them in the refrigerator, particularly in summer—mold prevention being the name of the game.

Commercially canned foods keep almost indefinitely, as long as the vacuum isn't broken. Unopened cans should be kept in a cool, dry place away from steam pipes and radiators and never near damp walls or floors.

For convenience, place cans with labels facing outward and store close to the point of first use. Door shelves can often be installed to hold small cans, and deep shelves can be adapted with stepped racks, wire racks, lazy susans, and pull-out bins that are available commercially for the purpose. Vinyl-covered wire racks permit you to see over and under stacks to the next layer and are desirable for high shelves that otherwise could not be inspected without a stepladder. A rotating shelf brings the back section to you. Pull-out shelves and bins for below-waist-level storage eliminate squatting and stooping.

STORAGE HINT: Don't discard the rinds of lemons, oranges, or other citrus fruits. Instead grate them, put in tightly covered jar and store in refrigerator. Use for adding a dash of flavor to appropriate dishes.

Home-canned goods (in jars, of course) are more perishable, but if properly "canned" they should hold up until the new crop comes in. A word of caution, however, to anyone who contemplates canning meat or vegetables: Obtain accurate instructions about procedures and temperature required to kill all microorganisms and enzymes. The rule varies according to the kind of food being processed. Botulism is a fatal food poisoning caused by a spore-forming bacterium sometimes present in food; once activated, the bacteria can be destroyed only by special processing and then with difficulty if at all. It also can show up in leftover cooked food that has not been refrigerated promptly. Canned foods generally should be refrigerated with dispatch as soon as they have been opened. Once the vacuum seal is broken, they are vulnerable to spoilage.

The can or jar itself may be the best container for storing foods in the refrigerator. Emptying a sterilized can of food into a container from the shelf may contribute to spoilage. It's a better practice to cover the open can for refrigerator storage. Acid foods (tomatoes, for instance) if left too long in the refrigerator, however, may take on a metallic taste from the can. This is harmless, but for long-term storage, empty contents into a small, properly washed container.

Storage life

Population explosions are too readily visible in certain foods, especially in the summer months in warm climates. Paprika is highly susceptible to infestation, and so are flour, corn meal, mixes, cereals, nuts, and dried fruits. Once infested, discard food immediately. Cold (refrigerator storage) and closed containers are your countermoves. Empty foods from cardboard containers to sturdy canisters or jars if your closets show signs of invasion.

The real cool

Potatoes and onions, including sweet potatoes, yams, garlic, and shallots, require a dark, cool, dry place with air circulation. If garlic buds tend to dry up before they are used, however, they may be transferred to a tight container in the refrigerator and kept almost indefinitely, or they can be separated into cloves, wrapped tightly in foil and frozen.

One of the repetitious but rather amusing advertising jingles of the recent past cautioned, with reason, never to put bananas in the refrigerator. The only exception to this would be to extend by a day or so the life of a fully ripe banana. Tomato flavor is equally overwhelmed and masked by refrigeration. Tomatoes should be stored in a brown paper bag to develop full flavor and chilled, if desired, just before serving, preferably not chilled through.

In general, most fruit of prime quality should be stored at room temperature for about five days after purchase; use fruits for centerpiece arrangements for an extra bonus of pleasure. Avocados, pineapples, mangos, and all the exotic fruits of the tropics make particularly charming centerpieces. A bowl of citrus fruit adds aroma as well as color to a room. When they begin to develop soft spots, transfer fruit and melons to the refrigerator or serve promptly.

The perishables

The most expensive part of the food budget is also the most perishable. Meat, in which you have the heaviest investment, fresh fruit and vegetables, milk and other dairy products all require refrigeration at varying temperatures. Our refrigerators have been engineered to provide optimum temperatures for each kind of food, along with the proper humidity. Don't defeat these objectives. The flowing moist cold in the crisper will prolong the life of salad greens for long periods of time; meat keeps best in the cold meat compartment.

Perishables should be refrigerated as soon as possible. Once perishables are stored, close the refrigerator door and open it as seldom as possible. Incidentally, a refrigerator door that swings wide each time it is opened indicates that the box needs leveling, in order for the magnetic catch to function.

Eggs lose food value and moisture through their shells. Latest research suggests that eggs be kept in a covered container in the refrigerator; egg-shaped shelves and racks on doors may be convenient but they are especially bad for eggs because eggs should not be jiggled. Eggs should be stored with the wide end up; this is where the air bubble is located, which should be kept intact.

Dairy fresh

Fresh dairy products need to be kept cold and tightly covered. Milk bottles or cartons should be dried and refrigerated. Cottage cheese, tightly covered, should be stored in the coldest part of the refrigerator. Hard cheese should be tightly wrapped to exclude air. Most will keep almost indefinitely, but wiping with a paper towel wrung out in a diluted solution of vinegar or storing in a "cheese keeper" retards mold. Should mold form, simply cut off the affected portion and then wrap the remainder.

Butter and margarine should be kept snugly wrapped and stored in a cold spot in the refrigerator until ready for use, and then kept in a covered butter dish. Fat drippings saved for cooking need to be covered and refrigerated. All fats and oils should be stored in containers with as little air as possible, since oxygen hastens rancidity.

Fresh produce

Fresh fruit and vegetables, except berries, should be washed and trimmed. Handle berries only enough to sort out and remove any damaged fruit. They should be stored dry and washed only just prior to serving.

Start washing fruit by filling a sink or large bowl with cold water. Wash apples, citrus fruit, and smooth-skinned vegetables first. Wash celery, scallions, radishes, and vegetables that have soil clinging to them last, changing the water as often as necessary. Sand will sink to the bottom. Very sandy vegetables should be agitated and left until the water is still, then lifted out without stirring up the sand. The process may take three or more rinses.

Slightly wilted greens will recrisp in a cold-water bath. Broccoli, celery, carrots, parsley, watercress, and leafy vegetables will freshen nicely if plunged for an hour or so into ice water to a depth at least two-thirds of their overall size. A practiced eye can judge at just what point slightly wilted vegetables at bargain prices are an economy.

Trim radish and scallion roots and tops and store the edible portions in ready-to-serve condition. Remove tops and root tips from carrots and beets to slow the sugar conversion in the roots. If beet tops are tender enough, wash and cook them separately. Corn keeps best in the moist husk, and beans and peas keep well in the pod—chill and use as soon as possible.

Remove tough outer leaves of salad greens and cabbage and discard them. Remove and keep tough outer stalks of celery, along with the tops of scallions, and add them to the stock pot. Crispers are so efficient that they keep even delicate salad greens for a week to ten days. Line the crisper drawer with several layers of paper towels to pick up the moisture. Use plastic sandwich bags to isolate the smell of scallions, garlic, and similarly aromatic foods, especially if the drawer is crowded.

Parsley and watercress will stay crisp several days if given their own special treatment. After washing and drying the greens thoroughly, gather them into a bunch, and crowd into a screw-top jar or other airtight container, or wrap snugly in a moisture- and vapor-proof plastic film. Parsley or watercress can sit in a little water in a jar in the refrigerator if it seems to need reviving, but as long as it's crowded into its own tight little world, it stays green and crisp for as long as a week. Plastic bags also work well for keeping other green vegetables crisp.

If your refrigerator space has to be stretched to store foods that are ordinarily placed in designated bins (fruits and vegetables with skins, oranges, green peppers, cucumbers, etc.), you should film-wrap them or drop them into plastic bags and close out the air by tying the ends of the bags. The air currents that prevent frost from forming in a refrigerator tend to dehydrate these foods quite rapidly if they are not covered.

Glass and plastic containers designed for refrigerator storage are convenient, practical, and attractive time-savers.

Fresh meat, fish, and chicken

Remove raw meats from the store's prepackage, rewrap them loosely in moistureproof paper, and store them in the meat compartment or the coldest part of your refrigerator. Some air circulation is desirable for fresh meat, but cured meat can be stored in the airtight prepackage. Ground meat and mechanically tenderized meat does not keep as long as roasts and steaks. Fresh poultry should be unwrapped, the giblets removed, and the cavity rinsed with cold running water. The bird can then be wrapped loosely, and stored in the refrigerator. Wrap giblets separately and keep them in the coldest spot or store in the freezer to collect for the stock pot.

Fresh fish should be unwrapped and rinsed under running water, and rewrapped loosely. Consult the care-and-use booklet that came with your refrigerator for directions on how long to keep food before cooking. In general, the newer your refrigerator, the longer fresh meats can be kept. Variety meats such as liver, kidney, and brains are especially perishable.

Smoked meats keep longer than fresh meats and uncut hams longer than ham slices. The more surface exposed to air, the more perishable is all meat, however.

Leftover meats should be cooled to room temperature and refrigerated promptly. Gravy, sauces, and custard that form a skin should be refrigerated with a piece of clear plastic wrap touching the surface.

A creative cook can make the second act of food performance more memorable than the first. Too often, especially with the beginning homemaker, the leftovers accumulate in bits and bowls, and after days in the refrigerator go to the garbage can. Keep a special section of one shelf in the refrigerator for leftovers—and a special place in your menus for their use. Keep vegetables and their cooking juices, meats, and bones for the stock pot or for casseroles or sauces.

The freezer compartment of the refrigerator should register 0° F. or lower. If it doesn't, it isn't a true freezer—it's an ice-cube-making compartment. A good test is how well it keeps ice cream, a difficult food to store except with a true freezer. Use the above-zero freezing compartment in a refrigerator for short-term storage, a great convenience for frozen-food cartons or to freeze for a week-at-most storage something that otherwise might go to waste.

Buying frozen foods

When a new food crop comes in, many stores offer frozen foods at astonishingly low cost. However, it is good to determine how these foods have been shipped and stored. Food loses quality rapidly as the temperature rises above 0° F. Large ice crystals form and break down cell structure. Meat can develop "freezer burn" and lose juices.

If a frozen food in the store has become shrunken in the package or if you can hear the crunch of large ice crystals as you squeeze it, the package has thawed somewhere in transit and been refrozen, with a resultant loss of quality. It might be well to test one package before stocking up. Should foods you buy accidentally defrost *partially* before you get them home, refreeze them; there will be only some loss of quality. Place in contact with a freezing surface, with plenty of air around them for a fast return to 0° F. Use within a few weeks.

If uncooked frozen food is completely thawed and warmed to room temperature use it immediately or, to be safe—especially if there is the slightest "off" odor—discard it. Never refreeze anything that was precooked, frozen, and thawed to room temperature unless you cook it *thoroughly* before refreezing, with the possible exception of breads and baked goods and concentrated juices.

In transit from the store to freezer, frozen foods need some protection. Ice cream is usually put in an insulated bag, but vegetables rarely are. Grouping the frozen foods in a double bag is a help; cover with a thick layer of newspapers as insulation. On days when you plan to stock the freezer, you might take along a blanket in the back of the car to cover the packages for insulation.

Pleasure of freezing

Your home freezer can be a true source of frozen assets if you use it wisely. Busy people, particularly working wives and live-alones, find a freezer their most effective ally in efficient meal-planning with limited shopping time. It is an exhilarating experience to buy several chickens for freezing, for example, at 10¢ a pound less than you are accustomed to paying; the savings potential becomes a reality when you put this to effective mealtime use, and it is wonderfully rewarding to have unexpected guests for dinner and be able to produce a masterful meal without strain.

You will discover that owning a freezer changes your way of life. The convenience of fewer marketing trips and the pleasure of cooking in quantity enable you to "program" your time with greater freedom and efficiency.

Save effort with a freezer by cooking double quantities of dishes (such as chili or cassoulet) that take long preparation, and store a "reserve meal" in the freezer. Bake in "doubles," too, and wrap a second cake for the freezer, saving for a rushed day or when guests drop in. In computing the value of a freezer, saved shopping time, car mileage, and cooking effort are plus factors not to be overlooked. It is especially satisfying to devote a rainy day to baking holiday cookies or preparing party canapes for the freezer.

While freezing can't improve food, it can retain freshness, color, and flavor. To improve the preservation of flavor and color by your own freezing technique, be sure to use proper moisture- and vapor-proof materials, packaging to exclude air as thoroughly as possible. Seal wraps with a double fold and plastic bags by twisting them closed, to exclude air, and freeze them immediately. Maintain 0°F. (or lower) and rotate foods so that recommended storage times are not exceeded. A Michigan State University study shows that a food that could stay at high quality for a year at 0°F. would keep well only two months if the temperature were raised to 10°F.

Rule of thumb decrees that no more food should be put in the freezer than can freeze in 24 hours; this is about 2 or 3

pounds of food to each cubic foot of capacity. Packages should
be placed on the freezing surfaces with room for the cold
to circulate in between. A severe overload of warm food raises
temperature, and food freezes too slowly to maintain quality.
It may even spoil.

The novice is likely to emphasize how long foods can be
kept in the freezer, but the efficiency and economy of the
freezer are adversely affected when foods are just kept and not
used. To get the most out of your freezer, you should plan its
contents and budget its space, keeping packages organized according to types of food and frequency of need.

Suggested maximum freezer storage times

Food	Storage time
FRUITS	10-12 months
VEGETABLES	10-12 months
MEATS	
Beef	10-12 months
Pork	4- 6 months
Veal	6- 8 months
Lamb and Mutton	8-10 months
Ground Beef	4- 6 months
Sausage, seasoned	2 months
Sausage, unsalted	4- 6 months
Ham	3- 4 months
Bacon, sliced	1 month (max.)
Bacon, unsliced	2- 4 months
Roasting Hens, Ducks, Capons, and Geese	12 months
Fryers and Broilers	12 months
Game Birds	6- 8 months
Fish; trout, bass, perch, sunfish, pike	6- 8 months
Variety Meats: liver, kidney, heart, tongue	1 month (max.)

DAIRY PRODUCTS AND EGGS

Cheese (hard)*	4- 5 months
Eggs (broken and mixed)†	10-12 months
Butter	4- 6 months
Cream	3- 4 months

BAKED PRODUCTS

Cakes, frosted	2 months
Cakes, unfrosted	3- 4 months
Pies, unbaked	1- 2 months
Pies, baked	1 month (max.)
Rolls and Bread	1 month (max.)
Cake Batter	2- 3 months
SANDWICHES	2- 3 months
SOUPS, STEW, CASSEROLES	1 month (max.)
LEFTOVERS (cooked)	1 month (max.)
ICE CREAM, original carton	1 month (max.)

* Soft cheeses do not freeze well.
† Break eggs into a bowl. Beat just enough to mix yolks and whites. Pack in liquid-tight containers.

Planning the use of freezer space

Stock foods your family likes best in quantities that are easy to use—meals for two, meals for four, and so on. Don't concentrate on commercially frozen foods or other readily available foods unless they happen to appear in the stores at an especially attractive bargain price. Guard against overstocking one food so that the next season's enticements won't find your freezer overcrowded.

As a guide to utilizing space, make a list of favorite foods and foods that require long preparation time, and estimate the quantity you would need to freeze to serve a month's needs. If you use your "standards" in rotation, this will leave plenty of room for storing seasonal foods.

Keeping an inventory

Label packages with contents and the date of stocking. Keep a list near the freezer. It can be on file cards or in a notebook or on a bulletin board or on a magnetized pad attached to the freezer. As packages are placed in the freezer, record the contents, size, date. As each gets used, the package notation can be crossed off.

After the newest packages have become thoroughly frozen, they can be stacked with other foods of the same kind, older packages being moved to the top and front so that they are used next.

The freezing center

Allocate some space near the freezer for the collection of materials you'll need for freezing: containers, wrappings, labels, waterproof pens or pencils, sealing tape, poultry shears, and similar needs.

Milk cartons or empty cottage-cheese cups can be used for freezing juices or for ice molds for punch bowls. They do not make satisfactory containers and are used mostly to shape a food that is being frozen; then the carton should be removed and the food wrapped in heavy foil or a heavy plastic bag.

To package food for the freezer, wrap food in the center of a generous piece of freezer wrap with about 3 to 4 inches overlap. Bring the long sides together in the center and fold over two times in 1-inch folds until it makes a good snug covering. Pressing the air out as you go, repeat with double folds on the two short ends. Seal with freezer tape and label with name, date, and weight. For easy separation of individual pieces, such as lamb chops or beef patties, insert a square of waxed paper between each piece. Then overwrap with freezer wrap as described above.

Space is needed in jars and containers for the expansion of the freezing process. Crumple freezer wrap in the top to minimize surface exposed to air while leaving expansion room. This is a good way to keep fruit from floating out of liquid.

Overwrap bread and other commercially baked goods or dairy

products only if long storage is anticipated. Such foods can be frozen in the wrappers they come in for a week or two. Small packets of fresh chopped herbs, onion, green pepper, celery, shredded cheese, and chopped nuts call for overwrapping for long storage. Mark each with identification and measured contents; date before freezing.

Here's a neat trick: Mold casseroles and other cooked foods over liners of foil or film in the dishes in which they are later to be reheated. When they are frozen, remove them; overwrap, tape, and label them; then return to the freezer. When you want to serve them they'll fit the dish they originally came out of.

How to freeze meat

Wipe meat with a damp towel to remove bone slivers. Separate steaks, chops, or patties with pieces of waxed paper (or wrap). Pad any sharp bones with thick folds of paper to prevent punctures in the outer wrapping. Place meat in center of a sheet large enough to be folded over three times in 1-inch folds until the paper is tight and as little air as possible is entrapped. Repeat for ends. Tape and label, giving kind, cut, weight, date, and number of servings.

How to freeze poultry

Whole birds: Remove pin feathers if present and rinse bird thoroughly in cold water inside and out. Lock wings in back and fold neck skin over. Tie legs and pad above ends to prevent puncturing the wrapping. Wrap in moisture- and vapor-proof material—paper, foil, or plastic film or bag—pressing out as much air as possible. Tape and label.

Poultry parts: Flatten pieces and separate with double thicknesses of wrapping. Pad sharp ends of bones with wrapping. Wrap or bag as instructed previously; tape and label. Note: Remember to clip wing tips, necks, and backs, and freeze them separately for stock.

Giblets: Package separately. Livers are somewhat more perishable and should be used within a month.

How to freeze fish

Fish from the market will be whole, filleted, or cut into steaks. To reduce the drip during thawing, give steaks and fillets a 30-second bath in a 5-percent brine solution before freezing— three tablespoons of salt to a quart of cold water. Fold the ragged ends of the fillet under, and for most attractive serving, shape, freeze separately, and then wrap. For whole fish and fish steaks, wrap and freeze separately or separate with double thicknesses of wrapping, and then wrap and freeze.

Fish caught by sports fishermen should not be allowed to flop around in the bottom of the boat and get bruised. They should be killed and dressed soon after being caught and the dressed fish iced or refrigerated until it can be packaged for freezing.

How to freeze oysters, clams, and scallops

Scrub as much sand as possible from shells, taking care not to introduce sand inside the shell during the shelling. The shucked shellfish, if very sandy, can be rinsed under a spray of water,

but this washes away flavor, unfortunately. Pack firmly and cover with 2½-percent brine solution (one-third cup salt to one gallon water).

Scallops can be frozen individually and packaged or packed into serving portions and separated by double thicknesses of wrapping.

How to freeze shrimp, crab, and lobster

Raw shrimp in their shells have a long keeping time. They should be washed and packed in 2½-percent brine solution (see above). They may be shelled and frozen in brine or cleaned and cooked before freezing. Cooked shrimp toughen somewhat when frozen, however.

Freeze either cooked meat from lobsters and crabs, or kill and clean live lobsters and freeze the meat raw.

How to freeze fruit

Select only top-quality fruit and prepare it for freezing just as soon as you get it home unless, as is usually true of such fruit as peaches, it needs time to ripen fully. If you really want to get serious about home freezing, write to the U.S. Department of Agriculture, Extension Service, Washington, D.C., for guides to specific varieties of fruit recommended for freezing.

Fruits can be frozen packed in syrup; packaged in granulated sugar or dry; or spread on a cookie sheet and frozen, then packed. Berries can be packed dry, and so can other small fruits for special diets, although they tend to lose some of their flavor. Light syrup is made by dissolving two cups of sugar in a quart of boiling water. Medium syrup uses three cups of sugar to a quart of boiling water. The syrup is made ahead of time and refrigerated. If sugar pack is your preference, it is usually in the ratio of one cup of sugar to four cups of fruit. Fruit packed in syrup is usually used for desserts; when packed dry in sugar or left unsweetened, it is usually used for cooking or serving just as it thaws.

Before packing, the fruit is washed in cold water, a small quantity at a time to avoid undue handling and bruising. A colander or wire basket is useful to lift fruit out of the water and drain it. Fruit should not stand in water; some fruits get waterlogged, while other fruits lose food value and flavor.

Prepare fruit for freezing much as you would for serving. Stem and remove pits, slice or section, peel or puree, and prepare according to whether pieces of fruit need to be cut in small pieces or crushed. Use any equipment—stainless steel, glass, aluminum, ceramic ware—but not galvanized metal ware; fruit acids dissolve the zinc, which is poisonous. Iron ware and tin ware with a thin plate may produce an unpleasant metallic taste and are best avoided.

Many fruits require the addition of acid to keep them from darkening. This can be ascorbic acid obtained from the drugstore in crystalline or powder form, citric acid or lemon juice (which contains both citric acid and ascorbic acid), or special freezing preparations.

Leave space when packaging fruit into containers. Crush freezer wrapping placed between the fruit and the cover helps keep pieces of fruit submerged while allowing for expansion while freezing.

How to freeze vegetables

The fresher the vegetables are when you freeze them, the better. Best of all are tender vegetables straight out of the garden and right into your freezer. Unless protected by pods—lima beans, green peas—they must be washed in cold water and lifted out after the sand and grit have settled.

Prepare vegetables as for cooking; peel, trim, and cut into uniform pieces or sort according to size for heating and packing.

Scalding or blanching is an important step in freezing vegetables to stop the growth of enzymes, and the heating time varies with the vegetable and the size of the pieces. A blancher is needed or a large kettle with a cover, holding at least a gallon of boiling water into which the vegetables can be dropped in a basket or wire sieve. Vegetables are heated for one, two, three, or more minutes and then plunged into ice water. Cooling takes about twice as long as the heating. Vegetables may then be packed dry; after blanching, they are slightly wilted and easier to pack. Keep in mind that vegetables also need head space for expansion in the process of freezing.

How to freeze eggs

Egg whites: To freeze, nothing need be added, but egg whites can be packaged either with salt or with sugar if desired. Freeze in ice-cube trays and package or fill containers, leaving head space, and label with date. Use within 12 hours of thawing.

Whole eggs: Gently mix and freeze—with salt for eventually scrambling or for omelets; with sugar for baking desserts. For each two cups of eggs add one teaspoon of salt or one tablespoon of sugar or corn syrup.

Egg yolks: Break them gently and mix thoroughly with either two teaspoons of salt or two tablespoons of sugar or corn syrup for each two egg yolks, but be careful not to whip in any air.

1⅓ tablespoons thawed yolk = 1 fresh egg white
2 tablespoons thawed egg white = 1 fresh yolk
3 tablespoons thawed whole egg = 1 fresh egg

How to freeze baked goods

Baked yeast bread and rolls: Very satisfactory for freezing. When cool, wrap and label. Defrost in wrapper at room temperature or, if foil-wrapped, in a 325°F. oven for 20 minutes. Sliced bread can be toasted without thawing—just takes a little longer.

Quick breads: They freeze well and thaw out like yeast bread. Popovers are best reheated at 400°F. for 10 minutes. Frozen waffles can be reheated in a pop-up toaster.

Cakes: All cakes can be frozen after cooling, but it is important to defrost them in the freezer wrapping. Gingerbread is improved if warmed slightly before serving.

Frosted cakes: Freeze unwrapped, supported on a piece of heavy cardboard covered with foil or waxed paper; then wrap or store in a large plastic bag. These, too, must be thawed in their wrappings. If necessary, use toothpicks at the corners to keep the wrapping just above the frosting. Tape ends of the toothpicks to prevent puncture of the wrapping. Butter, fudge, or penuche icings can be frozen satisfactorily.

Uncooked yeast dough and cake batter: Can be frozen for a time (preferably no longer than a month), but the dough will not rise so well as it would if you bake first and freeze afterward.

Baked cookies, rolled and cutout cookie dough: Separate with double thickness of waxed paper. Rolls of refrigerator cookie dough and drop cookies, frozen and then packaged, all produce good results from the freezer. Thaw baked cookies in their wrapping. Thaw rolled dough slightly before slicing to bake. Bake rolled and drop cookies without thawing.

How to freeze pies

Except for cream and custard pies and those with meringue tops, pies can be frozen either baked or unbaked, whichever is most convenient.

Unbaked pies: Prepare as usual, except that no steam vents are cut in the tops. Protect the top with a paper plate, wrap and freeze; or freeze first, then top with a paper plate, wrap and freeze-store. At baking time, cut the steam vents and bake frozen, allowing 15 to 20 minutes extra time. Unbaked fruit pies offer fresh-baked flavor with freedom to prepare in your own—or the fruit's—good time.

Baked pies: Wrap in foil when cooled, taking care to set juicy pies on a level shelf. To serve cold, defrost at room temperature for 1½ hours, or heat unwrapped in a 375°F. oven for 40 to 50 minutes. To counteract the tendency for the lower crust to become soggy during reheating, roll the crust thinner than usual and brush with melted fat or lightly beaten egg white before filling.

Chiffon pies: Chill until set, freeze, wrap, and return to the freezer. Thaw at room temperature about an hour or in the refrigerator 2½ to 3 hours.

Unbaked pastry: Roll in flat disks ready to use or store in bulk; or, unrolled, divided into balls for one- or two-crust portions. Roll disks of pastry 3 inches larger in diameter than the diameter of the pie plate for which they are destined. Place on foil-wrapped cardboard, separating disks with double thicknesses of waxed paper. Wrap in foil, or put in plastic bag and seal. Freeze shells in pie plates, remove, and stack with crumpled waxed paper between them. Place on cardboard, slip into plastic bag, and seal.

How to freeze main dishes and cooked foods

Pot roast, meat loaf, chili con carne, Spanish rice, chicken or turkey pie, a la king dishes, stuffed peppers, stuffed baked potatoes, French-fried potatoes, macaroni and cheese, casseroles, onion rings, baked apples, applesauce—all freeze well, as do most similar foods. Almost any standard recipe can be doubled to make a batch for the freezer.

Freezer bonuses: Foods that are to be reheated before serving should be slightly undercooked. Meat should be tender but firm, vegetables a little crisp to the fork. Cook them quickly. Package and freeze as soon as cooled.

- Seasoning is best kept light and adjusted when reheated. Pepper gets stronger and some herbs and spices change flavor in the freezer.
- Use a minimum of fat in sauces. A little will recombine when reheated, but fat separates during freezing.
- Don't freeze hard-cooked egg white—it toughens. Or potatoes—they turn mealy. Substitute rice or add potatoes at serving time.
- Freeze convenient serving amounts. Unless food is thawed before reheating, it's convenient to have it frozen to fit the pan or casserole.
- Plan to use cooked foods within a short time—two to three months.

- Most meat sandwiches can be frozen. Use a minimum of mayonnaise or salad dressing. Omit lettuce and crisp raw vegetables.

Tips for freezing plain and fancy foods

Prepare your party and holiday food in advance—and freeze. Freeze clown faces in ice cream balls for the children, fancy canapes and tea sandwiches for grown-ups.

- Bake cream puffs, big ones and bite-size, package, and freeze. Defrost and fill with cream, ice cream, chicken salad, potted meat spread or seafood-salad mixture.
- Pineapple art: Freeze a punch bowl surprise. To prepare, peel a whole pineapple, leaving the frond intact. Stud with whole strawberries stuck on toothpicks. Brush with clear corn syrup and freeze. Place, frozen, in the center of a champagne punch bowl for flavorful chill and charm.
- When you find big, beautiful mushrooms in the market, buy for freezing. Cut a thin slice off the stem, wipe caps and stems with a damp paper towel and freeze. To cook, slice while still frozen.
- Cut melon balls from firm, ripe cantaloupe, honeydew, and watermelon. Cover with light syrup (see How to freeze fruit) to which is added a few drops of peppermint and green food coloring. Garnish with fresh mint leaves.
- Party staples collected beforehand or leftovers from a party keep well in the freezer. Freeze shaved or crushed ice cubes, cubes frozen with maraschinos and mint leaves in them, coffee cubes, and other party tidbits. Potato chips, crackers, and pretzels can be bought in quantity, frozen in small suitable portions. Thaw them right in their wrappings. Even unsmoked leftover cigars and cigarettes can be wrapped and frozen for freshness.
- Prepare pumpkin puree in season, some for pies, some for cream of pumpkin soup—freeze.

- Collect herbs in season from the market or the garden. Mince and freeze, or freeze in bouquets.
- Cranberries need only to be washed and packaged. Freeze enough to last all year.
- Fruit cakes mellow beautifully in the freezer.
- Grate horseradish and freeze for sauce.
- Make regular trips to your favorite roadside market and buy fresh-picked fruits and vegetables. Then rush to your freezer.

Quantity preparation for the freezer

Every woman who owns—or wants—a food freezer dreams of opening the door to a stock of delicious home-prepared foods, wrapped, ready to heat, in some cases, right in the serving dish. Most women face one major problem in making this come true: finding the time or help to prepare food in large quantities.

One solution is to enlist the aid of a freezer cook, a person who can come in one day a week to help. The same idea might be used by a group of neighbors who set aside a certain day each week to help stock one another's freezers, taking turns first in one kitchen, then another, with each woman contributing her own specialties. Like old-time quilting bees, freezer days can be social fun.

With extra time or help, it's possible to freeze many different kinds of food in quantity: company dishes, sandwiches and other foods for the children's lunches, entrees of all types, desserts. Double recipes of favorite dishes can be prepared, then packed in individual or family-size servings to be used as needed. With a large freezer you can even freeze entire menus for parties of different sizes—ready to heat and serve at the last minute, as the need arises.

The following recipes incorporate kitchen efficiency, economy, and ease in the quantity preparation of freeze-ahead menus.

Barbecue sauce

Chop very fine 2 tablespoons **parsley,** 1 **onion,** 2 large cloves **garlic**; place in saucepan. Add I teaspoon **dry mustard,** 1 teaspoon **sage**, ½ to ¾ teaspoon **cayenne**, 1 tablespoon **paprika**, 1 tablespoon **Worcestershire sauce**, 2 teaspoons **sugar**, 3 tablespoons **olive oil** or **salad oil**, and 6 tablespoons **vinegar**. Into this pour 4 cans of **tomato sauce** (8 oz. each) and an equal amount of **water**; add **salt** and **pepper** to taste and simmer 45 minutes. Makes 8 cups. (You will need about 1 cup barbecue sauce for 4 pounds spareribs.)

Barbecued Spareribs

Allow ¾ pound of ribs per person for generous servings. Remove excess fat from 4 pounds of **ribs**, season with **salt** and **pepper**; lay on broiler rack so that ribs do not overlap, place 4 inches from heat. Broil ten minutes on each side or until very well browned. Remove, arrange in one layer in shallow baking pan or pans; pour over 1 cup of the **barbecue sauce** and bake in moderate oven (350°F.) about 40 minutes, turning and basting several times. Ribs are done when skin between them cracks. Cool; wrap well in aluminum foil to freeze. Remove from freezer several hours before serving. Place in moderate oven (350°F.) for 20 to 30 minutes. If not thawed, spareribs take about 40 minutes to heat.

Beef stew with cinnamon

Cut 2 pounds **beef stewing meat** into small cubes; brown meat in 2 tablespoons **salad oil** or **shortening**. As meat sizzles, finely chop all these: 1 bunch **scallions** or 1 medium **onion**, 3 or 4 stalks of **celery**, a few sprigs of **parsley** and ½ **green pepper**. Add chopped vegetables to meat along with a dash of **cayenne**, a dash each of **oregano** and **thyme** and ¼ teaspoon **rosemary**. Next add 1 large can (29 oz.) of **tomatoes** and 2 cans (8 oz. each) **tomato sauce.** Sprinkle ½ teaspoon **cinnamon** over the top. Stir just to blend ingredients, cover pot, bring to boil and let simmer for 2½ hours. Then add 3 small **carrots**, chopped, and simmer stew one haf-hour longer. Serves 10. Pack in small metal containers to use separately or together as needed.

Fried freezer chicken

Steam 2 **chickens** (2½ to 3 pounds each), cut up, in about 1 cup **salted water** for 20 minutes. Cool chicken. Beat 2 **eggs** slightly, add 1 teaspoon **salt.** Combine 1 cup **cracker crumbs** with 2 teaspoons **paprika.** Dip chicken pieces in egg, roll in cracker crumbs. The chicken is wrapped in individual pieces to avoid sticking together. (The stock left from steaming the chicken may be used for soup or sauces. It can be frozen, too.) To serve, remove from freezer and, while frozen, fry in deep, hot fat.

Quick cranberry relish

Pare the yellow rind from 1 large or 2 small **oranges.** Trim off and discard white membrane, cut oranges into several pieces and remove seeds. Put oranges, orange rind, and 1 pound **whole cranberries** (fresh or frozen) through food chopper, using medium blade. Add 1¼ cups **sugar,** mix well. Freeze.

Orange pudding cake

Into mixing bowl put ½ cup **shortening,** the grated rind of 2 **oranges** and 2 **lemons** and ½ teaspoon **salt;** blend well. Gradually add 1 cup **sugar,** creaming well. Add 1 **egg,** beat well. Add 2 cups **all-purpose flour** (sifted before measuring) alternately with 1 cup **buttermilk** or **sour milk,** which has been blended with 1 teaspoon **baking soda;** mix just until blended. Finally, stir in 1 cup **raisins.** Turn into greased baking pan (8 x 12 inches); bake in a moderate oven (350°F.) about 35 minutes. While cake bakes, combine ¾ cup **orange juice,** ¼ cup **lemon juice,** and 1 cup **sugar;** place over medium heat about 5 minutes. When cake has been removed from oven, pour mixture slowly over hot cake in pan. When cool, wrap cake, still in pan, with freezer paper, and store in freezer. To serve, thaw slowly at room temperature. Serve warm or cold with heavy cream or whipped cream.

Garlic French bread

Slice 1 large or 2 smaller loaves of **French bread** in half, lengthwise. Spread both cut sides generously with **butter,** flavored with crushed or finely chopped **garlic** (use about 1 garlic clove to each ½ cup butter). Put halves together again; make crosswise slashes in bread to about ½ inch of bottom of crust. Wrap in aluminum foil and place in freezer. To serve put foil-wrapped bread in moderate oven (350°F.) for 15 to 20 minutes if bread has been defrosted; takes about 25 minutes if bread is frozen.

Cream puffs

Sift and measure 1 cup **all-purpose flour,** add ½ teaspoon **salt;** sift again. In saucepan combine 1 cup **water** and ½ cup **shortening;** bring to vigorous boil over medium heat. Turn heat low; add flour all at once and stir vigorously over low heat until mixture forms ball and leaves side of pan. Remove from heat and add 4 unbeaten **eggs,** one at a time, beating thoroughly after each addition. Continue beating until thick dough is formed. For dessert-size puffs, drop by rounded tablespoonfuls onto greased baking sheet about 2 inches apart. Bake in hot oven (425° F.) for 25 to 30 minutes or until beads of moisture no longer appear. For appetizer-size puffs drop dough by teaspoonfuls onto greased cookie sheet and bake in hot oven (425° F.) for 12 to 15 minutes. Cool, cover or wrap well to freeze. Let thaw at room temperature or place in slow oven (325° F.) for about 15 minutes before filling.

Tangy meat loaf

Combine 2 cups **soft bread crumbs,** ⅓ cup **milk,** 1 **egg;** mix well. Add 2 tablespoons finely chopped **onion,** 1½ pounds **ground beef,** ½ pound **ground pork,** 2 teaspoons **salt,** ⅛ teaspoon **pepper,** 1 tablespoon **Worcestershire sauce,** and ⅛ teaspoon dried **basil** or **thyme;** mix thoroughly. Place in loaf pan or in shallow, oblong baking pan and bake for 1 hour in a moderate oven (350° F.); cool.

Sandwich fillings

Tuna Relish: To 1 can (6½ oz.) flaked **tuna**, drained, add 2 tablespoons **pickle relish**, 1 chopped **hard-cooked egg yolk**, 1 teaspoon **lemon juice**, and 2 tablespoons **mayonnaise** or **salad dressing**.

Ham and Cheese Spread: Combine 1 cup shredded **process American cheese**, 1 cup chopped **cooked ham** or **luncheon meat**, 2 tablespoons **catsup**, a dash **dry mustard**.

Cold storage at home

Here's a tip. If stored at home, furs, cashmere sweaters, and other woolens can be packaged for the freezer like food, frozen for 48 hours, and removed to a cool dry place without unsealing the wrapping. They will be moth-free until next season's generation of moths.

Frosted food limitations

While practically all foods can be frozen and stored in the freezer at 0° F. if properly packaged, there are a few exceptions to keep in mind. Crisp fruits and vegetables won't come out particularly firm, nor will vegetables with a high water content that you want to serve raw, though they can, of course, be used for cooking. Raw lettuce, celery, large tomatoes, and cucumbers do not freeze well either. Forget them. But if you come onto a large quantity of fresh ripe tomatoes, prepare as juice or puree for new fresh flavor, or stew or cook them into sauces and freeze pronto.

Chapter 5

How to streamline meal preparation

The average housewife spends 20 percent of her work hours in the kitchen preparing meals and cleaning up afterward. How much of this time is spent performing inefficiently, with wasted footsteps, difficult reaches, deep crouches, and contortions that would do credit to an acrobat? Research studies at Cornell University indicate that effective planning of equipment placement to save unnecessary motions can improve kitchen efficiency by 20 percent; forward-looking designers estimate that efficiency can be improved 50 percent by employing even more advanced kitchen concepts.

Kitchen scientists visualize the day when women will go to a home computer, indicate the meal mood and the participants, and then sit back while the programmed unit selects the ideal choice of foods, routes them to heating or chilling units, onto plates, and onto the table. After the meal, plates will be electronically cleaned and stored or discarded. Ah, brave new kitchen world!

Meanwhile, more immediate practicalities can make meal planning a personal adventure.

Cooking in three-quarter time

Researchers concerned with energy expenditure and optimum kitchen productivity point to the importance of a continuous flow of movement and completion of tasks without interruption. This applies to cooking, too.

- *Cook once—serve twice.* Prepare such basics as potatoes, rice, or spaghetti sauce in double quantity. Today's mashed potatoes may be tomorrow's Vichyssoise; leftover boiled rice is transformed into fried rice or Arroz con Pollo; extra spaghetti sauce flavors a casserole of Eggplant Parmesan, or makes a quick pizza.

- *Keep a stock pot going.* Begin with broth cooked from bones and bouquet garni and strained, or simply start with a prepared broth. Cut up and add leftover meats, bits of vegetables, pasta, potatoes, tomato sauce, that good dab of gravy, a few cut mushrooms, a ripe tomato seeded and diced. Such a pot, carefully developed, can transmute the tag ends of your meals to delicious soups, stews, and chowders almost effortlessly. Store in the refrigerator; if the pot stands a few days without use, bring to a boil and then let cool. Return it to the refrigerator until you need it.

- *Dips and spreads.* Collect these as you use cheeses. Blend pieces of sharp cheese with an equal amount of butter or margarine, moisten with brandy or wine, and keep the crock going indefinitely for party or snack readiness.

- *Meals a la carte.* Whether you store reserve supplies in the freezer or on shelves, assemble in one place all the elements of complete meals for different occasions, different groups—to meet any unexpected arrivals with aplomb.

- *Cook in the swing.* Make your own syncopation of dishes. Buy eggplant when you bring home a leg of lamb—and you are prepared with the makings of Moussaka. Prepare lentils when you know you will have a ham bone; or buy sour cream to blend with onion soup. Think of the flow and rhythm of your meals as you shop and cook. You'll save time and money all along the line and increase your family's eating pleasure in the bargain.

Plan menus carefully

The steady meat-and-potatoes routine is passé. Your family will welcome a change of pace, an all-in-one casserole, a hearty main dish, soup or salad, a skillet meal, an international specialty. Consider trying at least one new dish each week. If you have a freezer or large freezer compartment, out-of-season specialties or sauces or main dishes or desserts previously prepared add variety to menus and conserve effort, too. A roast cut into strips makes Sukiyaki as well as sandwiches; diced or minced, it can be used for stuffed mushrooms, as well as hash.

When planning a meal, decide on the main dish first; vegetables next; dessert last. If the main course is to be salad or soup, you'll want a hearty dessert, a pie or a cobbler, or a cake. But if you're planning a pot roast and potatoes, you'll need something light like a gelatine dessert. Round out the meal with the extras—bread or rolls served hot or cold, relishes, or other touches. Make a final check. The dishes in a well-planned menu do not clash in flavors, texture, or color, but do include contrasts. More important, a menu should be balanced to provide the foods you need in the right amounts:

Vegetable-Fruit Group	Includes all vegetables and fruits. This group is counted on to supply nearly all the vitamin C needed, and more than half the vitamin A.	Four or more servings, including 1 serving of a high vitamin C food (citrus fruit), and 1 serving of a good source of vitamin A (dark green or deep yellow vegetable).
Milk Group	Includes dairy products: milk, cheese, and ice cream. Milk is leading source of calcium; also provides high-quality protein, ribo-flavin, vitamin A.	Two or more 1-cup servings for adults; 3 to 4 servings for children.

Meat Group	Includes beef, veal, lamb, pork; poultry and eggs; fish and shellfish; also dry beans, lentils, nuts. Provides large amounts of protein, small amounts iron, thiamine, riboflavin, and niacin.	Two or more servings.
Bread-Cereal Group	Includes all breads and cereals that are whole grain, enriched or restored. Provides worthwhile amounts of protein, iron, B-vitamins, and food energy.	Four or more servings.
Other Foods	Not specified in above groups: butter, fats, oils, sugars. Supply calories and can add to total nutrients.	

Collect recipes wherever you go and index them on 3 x 3 cards. If you have favorites in cookbooks, note the page numbers and titles on cards in proper sequence. After you've managed to get a small collection together, classify it in groups to make locating recipes easy. No matter how much meal-planning experience you've had, you'll enjoy your preparations more if you have the stimulation of new ideas to plan with—and so will your family.

Organize work

You're off to a good start if you assemble all ingredients and utensils before you begin a job. A tray is a motion-saver for gathering things and keeping them in one spot. Study your own motions as you go through a familiar task. Establish the habit of using both arms and hands for greater efficiency, and work within an easy-reach arc to complete one set of activities before moving to another.

You'll save time if you combine or dovetail jobs during food preparation. Learn to do two things at once—it's a challenge! Bake cakes or cookies for dinner while washing the breakfast or luncheon dishes. Pare vegetables while meat is browning.

Schedule preparation and cleanup so that you can make use of every minute that you are in the kitchen.

Plan and organize the rest of your household schedule while you are in the kitchen. Peeling potatoes is detail work, but you can organize other things mentally while doing it. Try to alternate sit-down with stand-up work; don't be on your feet too long. Let your family help you. A chore that is routine or dull for you can be fun for a child if it is presented as a game. Young children can set the table. Older ones can help with the cooking and cleanup and be given the responsibility to complete each assigned task. Vary your assignments for each.

Be comfortable

Stand erect. Good posture prevents fatigue. Have sink, work table, countertops at heights that are comfortable for you. Your elbow is the measuring point for comfort. Counters should be 3 inches below your elbow height, the ideal height for comfort and kitchen efficiency. This is also the best height for the rim of the sink and the cooking surface of the range. The edge of your fully opened, down-swinging oven door should be 1 to 7 inches below your elbow in height; counter or pull-out boards for cake mixing, chopping, and beating should be 6 to 7 inches below elbow height. Adjust heights for specific chores for efficiency. If the dishpan is too low, for instance, place something under it for more comfortable working.

Begin the day bright. Dressing for kitchen work as you would for a job does wonders for your morale and for your family's, too. Wear comfortable shoes and clothing while working. Set your kitchen to music and chores will seem less burdensome. When you have a spare moment, sit down, close your eyes, and relax—or do a full stretch.

How to use a cookbook

No recipe, no matter how superb, will give successful results if you do not follow it with reasonable care. Here are some tips on how to use a recipe.

First read a recipe completely through. Then check the ingredient list. An experienced cook can make certain substitutions, but a novice had better stick to the rules. Do you have the proper utensils, including the right size pan? Can you complete preparation and cooking in time to serve?

Check the number of servings before you start. Each recipe will tell you the yield or average number of servings. Remember that these are servings. If second or third helpings are the rule in your family, increase the servings by increasing the ingredients proportionately. Besides, appetites differ greatly, and what may be ample for four people in one family may be barely enough for two people in another. The rest of the menu also makes a difference. An entree that follows an appetizer or a soup need not be so plentiful as a stew that is a one-dish meal in itself. Within your own family you will have learned these differences and be able to plan accordingly. When entertaining, however, it's always better to have too much than too little. If you are having six for dinner, choose recipes with a yield of at least eight or ten servings so that you can offer seconds (or multiply recipe ingredients to get the desired yields).

Follow directions carefully. Keep the book propped up and the page held open, so that you can refer to the recipe as many times as necessary. Take note of all directions—every word is there for a purpose. When preparing a meal for guests, always choose recipes that you have tried out at least once. This is not the time to experiment with an unfamiliar dish. Post your menu and recipes near the work center on a pegboard or bulletin board, or post it at eye level with magnet or tape. This will help you remember to serve those planned little extras such as sauces, preserves, condiments, and relishes. There is nothing as

---

MEAL-PREPARATION TIP: Not enough time to bake a cake for supper? Make cupcakes instead. Remember that it usually takes an hour or more to bake a loaf cake; 35 to 40 minutes for an oblong sheet cake; 25 to 30 minutes for layers; only 15 to 20 minutes for cupcakes or thin layers.

useless as a salad discovered in the refrigerator after the party is over!

Meals on tap

The secret of preparing a meal ready in minutes is twofold. Have on hand the ingredients you need to compose a complete menu in short order, and precook any parts of the meal you can. Restaurants cook roasts to the rare stage a day in advance. You can just as easily prepare a roast of beef or chicken or veal or lamb to the rare stage on the weekend or when you have time, then take it out of the refrigerator and finish cooking it to the desired degree before serving. Accompany this with quick-cooking rice or instant potatoes and fast-cooking vegetables, and you can have a meal on the table in minutes, starting from scratch.

Take advantage of such quick-cooking specialties as veal scallopine, fish and seafood, Braciola (thin-sliced beef strips), and, of course, steaks, chops, and old reliable ground meat to use in a dozen different ways. It pays to think in terms of complete menus as you shop for the makings of quick meals.

When you decide what you will have, begin with the part of the meal that takes the longest to finish and dovetail the other dishes into its time span as you work. If something is to be boiled in water, fill the kettle and start the water heating. When you go to the refrigerator, remove all the perishables you will need and set them close to the preparation area. Start the dish that will take longest to cook or heat, then clean faster-cooking vegetables and put the salad together. Set the table while everything's cooking. If possible, allow a few minutes to relax between the end of meal preparation and serving; change roles from cook to diner, and you will enjoy your own meal more, whether you eat it from a formally laid table or from an attractively set tray.

Since dinner is probably of greatest importance to the single person, let's watch three different girls as they come home to their respective apartments at the end of a long day. Note the difference efficiency in motion—and emotion—can have on the preparation of a quick meal.

Dotty comes home tired, decides she'll have a frozen macaroni casserole, salad, fruit, and coffee. She prepares the salad, boils water for coffee, takes a casserole from the freezer—and realizes it requires 45 minutes to heat. Puts it back in the freezer, falls off to sleep tired and hungry.

Janey walks into her apartment and decides to have a simple meal—tomato juice, steak with mushrooms, baked potatoes, frozen peas, tossed salad, red wine, strawberries, ice cream, and coffee. She takes out a glass of juice and drinks it before she begins. The drink awakens her appetite, and she puts a steak in the oven to broil; then realizes she can't broil the steak until the potato is at least half baked. Turns off the steak to bake the potato and mixes herself a drink. Decides to pan-fry the steak, then discovers, as it finishes, that the peas are still frozen. Turns off the steak while the peas cook, heats the steak again, gives up on the mushrooms, and sits down to her main course. Later she reaches into the freezer for the strawberries, decides not to wait while they thaw, has plain canned peaches with her coffee instead and wishes she had eaten out, as she faces the cold, stained broiler, skillet, and saucepan.

Betsy begins with somewhat the same plan but plays the game differently. She goes into the kitchen and turns the broiler on to preheat. Then she goes to the freezer, and removes the strawberries she intends to use and puts them under tap water to speed thawing—elapsed time *one minute*. Next she goes to the refrigerator to remove perishables, and finds half a cup of clam dip left over from last night's hors d'oeuvres. Whirls it in the blender with some tomato juice, for a quick clam bisque, empties it into a bowl, and fills the blender container with water to soak—this takes *two minutes*. Sprinkles the steak with seasoned tenderizer, lets it stand a few moments while she slices some mushrooms, which she drops into French dressing. Measures quick-cooking rice into a cook-and-serve pan and adds cold water, salt, and peas, plus a tablespoon of butter—*three more minutes*. While this is coming to a boil, she puts water on for coffee, pops the steak under the broiler, and prepares the salad —*six minutes*. Turns the steak, adds the mushrooms to brown, removes the rice and peas from heat to stand covered, and sets

the table—*five more minutes.* Now she decides to have the
strawberries Romanoff style, so she puts some sweet cream into
the beater bowl, and flips this on for a minute while she carries
in the bread, butter, bisque, and salad. Returns to the kitchen
to blend cream with ice cream, adds a dollop of Cointreau, and
folds in the berries—*three minutes.* Now she carries in the steak
and Risi Pisi, and settles down to uncork the wine and enjoy a
meal worth relishing, 20 minutes after she has arrived home.

And when the meal is over, her cleanup is simplified. Her
pans are all coated with easy-wash Teflon!

Know your flours

A ceramist at the potter's wheel, a handweaver at the loom, a
smith at the anvil, a woodturner at the lathe—every craftsman
who takes pride in producing a successful product knows his
materials cold. Essential to quality meal production in the kitchen
is your own thorough familiarity with the ingredients of foods.

All-purpose flour is milled from a selected blend of both hard
and soft wheats. It can be used for all types of baking and cooking.

Instant flour is all-purpose flour that has been so refined that
presifting is not necessary. For sauces, the flour can be added
directly to liquids without lumping. For baking purposes, it is
best to follow the manufacturer's directions.

Cake flour is made from highly refined soft wheat. It is ideal
for cakes, but not recommended for other baking purposes.

Bread flour is milled from hard winter wheat, which is higher
in protein, and has a higher gluten content than all-purpose flour.
This is the type used by commercial bakeries for chewy breads.

Self-rising flour is all-purpose flour or cake flour to which
leavening agents and salt have been added in the proper proportions for baking. Follow package directions carefully. This
type of flour should not be used in making yeast breads.

Whole wheat or *graham flour* is milled from hard wheat
with bits of the whole grain retained. It should not be sifted.
It is used in making breads, rolls, quick breads, other baking
products.

Soy flour and *rice flour* are usually found only in health food stores and should be used according to manufacturer's directions. Both of these flours are often used in combination with wheat flour because they lack gluten-forming properties. Waxy rice flour acts as a stabilizer in sauces and gravies.

Rye flour is the finely ground product of sifted rye meal, available in white, medium, and dark. It is usually combined with wheat flour in making bread.

Bleached flour has been sifted numerous times by the manufacturer to remove all bits of crushed whole grain and has been further processed to whiten the flour and make it more uniform. Use as an all-purpose baking and cooking flour.

Unbleached flour is white flour that has been refined but not put through the bleaching process. Use as an all-purpose flour.

Enriched flour is white flour, bleached or unbleached; the vitamins and minerals that were contained in the whole wheat grain have been restored. Use as an all-purpose flour.

Know your other grain products

Regular white rice has the hulls, germ, outer bran layer, and most of the inner bran removed.

Brown rice has had only the outer hull removed.

Long-grain rice is the best variety of rice for making casseroles or for simple steamed rice. Short- or medium-grain rice is suitable for puddings or other dishes that call for a soft product.

Converted rice has been cooked before milling by a special steam-pressure process that retains some of the vitamins in the interior of the brain. Parboiling gelatinizes the starch and thereby alters the cooking characteristics.

Precooked ("instant") rice is packaged long-grain rice that has already been cooked and needs only to steep or cook in boiling water for 5 minutes.

Wild rice is not rice at all, but the hulled grain of a water plant that has not been milled. It needs more cooking time than rice.

Corn meal is made by grinding white or yellow dried field corn.

Cornstarch is the refined starch of the dried corn kernel.

Hominy is corn with the hull and germ removed, left whole or broken into particles. Hominy grits are broken grains.

Oatmeal is available as regular and quick-cooking rolled oats. Regular oats and quick-cooking oats differ only in thinness of flakes.

Instant oatmeal is oatmeal that has been cooked, rinsed, and dried by a patented process. It needs only a short preparation time.

Tapioca is made from flour obtained from the cassava root. Flavored tapioca pudding mixes are blends of quick-cooking tapioca, cornstarch, sugar, and flavorings.

Bulgar is whole wheat that has been cooked and dried, with some of the bran removed, then cracked into coarse fragments. It may be used as a substitute for rice in many dishes, and sometimes it is called wheat pilaf.

Cracked wheat is prepared by cracking or cutting cleaned wheat, other than durum, into angular fragments.

Farina is made from wheat, other than durum, with the bran and most of the germ removed. It is prepared by grinding and sifting the wheat to granular form.

Wheat germ is the fat-containing portion of the wheat kernel. The germ is flattened and then sifted out as a yellowish, oily flake.

Know your sugars and syrups

Granulated white sugar has been refined from sugar beets or sugar cane. It is variously branded "granulated," "fine granulated," or "extra-fine granulated."

Superfine granulated sugar is a specially processed, uniformly fine grain sugar used in cakes and in mixed drinks and for other purposes where quick creaming or rapid dissolving is desirable.

Powdered or confectioners sugar is pulverized sugar used in frostings and icings and for dusting pastries, doughnuts, and other foods. It usually contains a small amount of cornstarch to prevent caking.

Brown sugar is not completely refined and contains varying quantities of molasses. It is variously designated as "light brown," "dark," "old-fashioned," indicating the color characteristic. Intensity of molasses flavor increases with color. Brown sugar imparts flavor and color to candies, baked goods, and the like.

Granulated brown sugar has uniform, fine-grain quality. It remains free-flowing and will not pack as regular brown sugar does. Volume is greater than that of regular brown sugar.

Molasses is the liquor from which raw cane sugar has crystallized. Table molasses is light in color and contains a higher percentage of sugars and a smaller percentage of ash than is present in cooking molasses. Cooking molasses is darker in color.

Maple syrup is made by boiling maple sap tapped from maple trees, concentrating it to a syrup. Most "maple syrups" sold in grocery stores are diluted (7–8% pure). Pure maple syrup is rare and expensive.

Corn syrup is obtained from cornstarch. Two types are commonly marketed. Light corn syrup has been clarified and decolorized. Dark corn syrup is a mixture of corn syrup and refiners' syrup; it is used both as a table syrup and for cooking purposes where its darker color and more distinctive flavor are desirable.

Honey is the nectar of plant flowers, gathered and concentrated by honeybees. For cooking purposes, the honey has been extracted from the honey comb, strained, and clarified.

Blended syrup is a mixture of different types of syrups. Composition of a blended syrup is indicated on the label.

Know your leavening agents

Baking soda is sodium bicarbonate. When combined with an acid ingredient (sour milk, molasses, sour cream), it releases carbon-dioxide gas, causing cakes and breads to rise.

Baking powder is a mixture of baking soda, acid salts, and starch or flour. (In low-sodium diets, baking powder with potassium bicarbonate rather than sodium bicarbonate can be used.) Baking powders vary according to their acid components—double-acting baking powder is now used extensively and is generally indicated in standardized recipes.

Yeast is a commercial product containing a microscopic cell of a benevolent fungus that (under suitable conditions of moisture, temperature, and nutrients) releases carbon dioxide for leavening breads and other yeast dough products. It comes in two forms, compressed yeast and active dry yeast.

Know your fats and oils

Margarine is made by emulsifying refined oils with cultured milk to produce a consistency similar to that of butter. All-vegetable oils or a mixture of animal fats and vegetable oils may be used in margarine. Some margarines have butter-flavoring materials added; salt is optional.

Vegetable oils are prepared from the seeds or fruits of a plant (corn, olive, peanut, soybean, cottonseed) by squeezing out the oil under heavy pressure.

Vegetable shortening is essentially solidified vegetable oils—corn oil, cottonseed oil, soybean oil, and peanut oil. The vegetable oils are refined and bleached, then hydrogenated to change the oil from a liquid to a solid state.

Lard is fat rendered from the fatty tissue of pork. It may be smooth or slightly grainy, depending on the manufacturer's treatment. Refined steam-rendered lard makes up most of the lard on the retail market.

Know your dairy products

Whole milk is fresh, sweet, and is generally pasteurized for human consumption; that is, it has been subjected to temperatures no lower than 145° F. for no less than 30 minutes (or a higher temperature for a shorter time) and then promptly cooled to 40° F. or lower.

Homogenized milk is pasteurized milk that has been mechanically treated to reduce the size of the milk fat globules. This stabilizes the emulsion so that fat does not separate into cream.

Skim milk is milk from which most of the fat has been removed.

"Chocolate milk," purchased commercially, is whole milk to

which sugar and chocolate have been added. If cocoa is added, it is designated as chocolate-flavored milk. "Chocolate drink" is made from skim milk or milk containing less milk fat than the legal minimum for pasteurized milk, using the same flavoring ingredients as in chocolate milk. If cocoa is added, it is designated as "chocolate-flavored drink."

Buttermilk is the product that remains when fat is removed from milk or cream in the process of churning.

Clabber is milk that has soured to the stage where a firm curd has been formed, but not to the point of separation from the whey, which is the watery part of milk.

Yogurt is a custard-like preparation made by fermenting concentrated whole milk with a special culture. Fruit or other flavors may be added.

Evaporated milk is whole cow's milk from which about 60 percent of the water has been removed. It is homogenized to distribute the fat globules uniformly in the milk, sealed in cans, and sterilized; or sterilized and aseptically canned. It may be fortified with vitamin D.

Sweetened condensed milk is the product resulting from the evaporation of about half the water from whole milk and the addition of refined cane and/or corn sugar in amounts sufficient for preservation, usually about 44 percent. It is heated and cooled before canning.

Dry whole milk (dry milk solids) is the product resulting from removal of water from whole milk. It contains not less than 26 percent milk fat and not more than 5 percent moisture.

Nonfat dry milk is the product resulting from the removal of fat and water from milk. It contains not more than 5 percent moisture and not more than 1.5 percent fat by weight. Most nonfat dry milk on the market is "instant," a form that has been treated to dissolve readily in water.

Cream is the milk-fat portion of milk that rises to the surface of milk on standing or which is separated from it by centrifugal force.

Light cream is coffee or table cream. It contains at least 18 percent milk fat.

Heavy cream is heavy whipping cream that contains not less than 36 percent milk fat, usually 36 to 40 percent.

Half and half is a product consisting of a mixture of milk and cream. It usually contains between 10 and 12 percent milk fat.

Pressurized whipped cream is a mixture of cream, sugar, stabilizers, and emulsifiers that are packed in aerosol cans under pressure. The cream is whipped when a gas dissolved in the cream is released through a nozzle.

Sour cream is cream to which a lactic acid culture has been added and allowed to ripen.

Butter is made from sweet or sour cream and contains not less than 80 percent milk fat. A lactic acid culture may be added to the cream for a short ripening period before churning, to develop desirable aroma and flavors. The addition of coloring and salt is optional.

Whipped butter is the product resulting from stirring or whipping butter with air, thereby increasing its volume and making it easier to spread.

Cheese is the curd of milk separated from the whey and prepared in many forms and in a wide variety of flavors and textures. In the United States the most common cheese is cheddar, which is sold both colored and uncolored.

Natural cheese is made from cow's, sheep's, or goat's milk or cream and is usually cured or aged for a specific period to develop flavor. Natural cheese (from soft to very hard cheese) is classified by texture or consistency and degree or kind of ripening.

Process cheese is pasteurized cheese made by blending one or more lots of cheese into a homogeneous mass with the aid of heat, water, and an emulsifier.

Cheese spreads are somewhat similar to process cheeses except that a stabilizer is used, the moisture content is higher, and the milk-fat content is lower. Spreads may be flavored by adding chopped pimento, olives, onion, or similar foods.

Ice cream is prepared by freezing while stirring a pasteurized mix composed of milk, cream, sugar, stabilizers, and various flavorings such as extracts, fruits, chocolate, or nuts. Coloring may have been added. Eggs may also have been added as an optional ingredient. The milk-fat content ranges from 8 to 14 percent, usually 10 to 12 percent for plain ice cream, although some special ice cream may be as high as 20 percent fat.

Ice milk is made in the same manner as ice cream and uses the same ingredients, but in different proportions. The milk-fat content is usually much lower, ranging from 2 percent to approximately 7 percent. It may be sold in either soft- or hard-frozen form.

Sherbet is prepared by freezing a pasteurized mix of sugar, milk solids, stabilizer, food acid, and water; fruits, fruit juices, and extracts are added as flavoring ingredients. Federal standards specify that the milk-fat content of sherbet must be between 1 and 2 percent and the total milk-solids content between 2 and 5 percent.

Know a few other things about food

Unsweetened chocolate is pure chocolate made by grinding cocoa beans that have been roasted and shelled. It is a general-purpose cooking and baking chocolate. When called for in a recipe without further description, the term chocolate means unsweetened chocolate.

Sweet chocolate is chocolate mixed with sugar and may also contain added cocoa butter and flavorings. It is used in all-purpose cooking as well as for dipping confections.

Semisweet chocolate pieces or squares are formed from partially sweetened chocolate. They are usually used whole in baking or eaten as a confection.

Cocoa is powdered chocolate from which a portion of the cocoa butter has been removed. Breakfast cocoa is a high-fat cocoa that must contain at least 22 percent cocoa fat.

Instant cocoa is a mixture of cocoa, sugar, and an emulsifier. It can be prepared for use without cooking by adding hot liquid.

Coconut, flaked or grated, is coconut meat cut into uniform shreds or flakes.

Gelatin is obtained from collagen in bones and skin of animals by hydrolysis. When called for in a recipe without further description, it means the unflavored type.

Fruit-flavored gelatin is a mixture of plain gelatin, sugar, fruit acids, flavors, and coloring.

Olives, the edible fruit of the olive tree, are available in cans or jars as ripe olives, green fermented, or green brined olives. Both green and ripe olives are treated to remove the characteristic bitterness of the nut.

White distilled vinegar is made by the fermentation of distilled alcohol. It is clear in color and can be used as an all-purpose vinegar, but is especially good for pickling and preserving.

Cider vinegar is made from the fermentation of apple juice. It is a general-purpose vinegar, has a golden hue, and is the most widely used vinegar in cooking.

Wine vinegar is made from the alcoholic fermentation of the juice of grapes. It is particularly popular for salad dressings.

Chapter 6

How to set a table for any occasion

Primitive man ate meat from the bone. As he acquired a measure of grace, he invented tools and utensils, among the first of which were the shell and the sharp-edged stone, which early man chipped to make sharper. Ancient Greek and Roman serving vessels were intricate and ornate, but the hand was the eating tool.

In Elizabethan times, Rosencrantz and Guildenstern commented on the "new invention" of forks in Italy as a device to keep fingers unsoiled. Cardinal Richelieu had silversmiths blunt the edges of table knives for safety's sake. Before that, the hunting weapon had been brought to the table, its sharp edge turned inward toward the plate for safety's sake.

As silversmiths evolved fine flatware, style predominated over utility, with the fish fork, the lemon fork, the pickle fork, the luncheon fork, the dinner fork, the salad fork, the serving fork, the carving fork—and by Victorian times ladies were handling this array of silver service with gloved fingers! Through it all, some practicality remained, however. Tables were set so that the first piece of silver required was the closest at hand.

Tablesetting is a kind of social communication. It calls attention to a special occasion, adds cheer to any morning, warmth to any winter evening. The message is the mood established for the meal. The medium is the way the table is set to serve that meal. As in all kinds of communication, this one has its rules. These have become greatly simplified in our time.

Matching sets of dishes, special glassware for each course, and white damask tablecloths are no longer the order of the day. Young brides are more often concerned with finding shelf space for books or techniques for quick meal preparation after work or school than with assembling a perfectly matched set of table accessories. Imagination and a sense of design is the new approach to tablesetting, with the emphasis more on care than cost.

Homemakers have discovered the joys of collecting unusual groups of dishes and serving pieces to set off special meals. Colorful French Quimper plates, for example, bring sunshine to the breakfast table whatever the weather outdoors. A flowered sheet makes the perfect tablecloth for a summer supper and is as likely to be found in homes of affluence as in homes where improvisation counterbalances budget limitations.

Contemporary families have little time together, and when the family eats together at mealtime this may be the only hour when the family communicates as a group. Even if the children come to the table in jeans, they react to a gracefully set table. A child asked to pick a bouquet or arrange a centerpiece or draw place cards is made to feel a part of the goal of making the meal a success. Each incipient host and hostess will grow up knowing how to set a table.

Tablesetting is an art in which your eye, your sense of line and design, reflect the way your family lives. Plan your table for comfort and ease of serving. Plan it for beauty and to give your family and guests a sense of well-being.

Everyday tablesetting

In many ways the simple meals are the most fun to set up. Holidays and birthdays should be special; tablesettings have a way of becoming family traditions. A heart at each setting says Valentine's Day. A Christmas music box can hold a generation of red candles and have the holly trim replaced many times. If that is the way children remember being called to Christmas dinner, it will bring magic to the meal.

If you like bright color, the new hot hues are a good background for food. You can begin with brightly flowered or colored cloths and contrasting napkins. Stark white or solid-color china will set off the background.

The rules for tablesetting are constantly changing. Traditionally, white damask covered the table, and napkins were matching white damask, polished and crisp, without a trace of a wrinkle. This is still the most formal cloth—*if* you want the most formal. Pale damask, considered almost but not perfectly correct, is generally limited to better restaurants and hotel dining rooms. The formal table, like the formal invitation, sometimes marks an occasion, but the rest of the time most of us enjoy a more vital, creative approach to tablesetting.

Tablecloth techniques

You can lighten your laundry load without lessening the charm of your table. Use mats of washable materials and make the most of washer-to-dryer-to-table fabrics. To iron a cloth or touch up wrinkles readily, place it over felt, and iron on the table, or set your board close to the table, and slide the cloth onto the table as you finish.

Make the most of decorative fabrics for cloths and napkins. It isn't necessary to buy table linens exclusively in the linen department. A summer luncheon may be coolly inviting on a brightly flowered mint-green dressmaker fabric. Sheets in floral and geometric fabrics are frequently used as table covers by photographers who create magazine photographs.

Pastel colors are a change of pace. If it pleases your fancy, there is every reason in the world to use garnet-red felt when you're serving roast beef and Yorkshire pudding. A strip of wide lace down the center of the table can heighten the Edwardian effect. Colorful inexpensive felt in any of its many colors, simply cut to table size, regular or floor length, sets off party tables to advantage, and even covers improvised tables elegantly. Dry-clean felt tablecloths between uses.

A tablecloth seems to make for a less cluttered table for a big meal with lots of food and many people. Place mats disturb the visual continuity of the table and create a feeling of separation instead of group participation. On the other hand, at a small breakfast or luncheon table, place mats have the opposite effect.

Vary the look of the table. An original, attractive setting, no matter how basic or how simple, seems to make the food taste better. Keep in mind the mood of the occasion. A too-formal table may embarrass casually dressed guests, but a strictly formal gathering requires comparable table preparation.

Silver, china, and glassware

The patterns of your flatware, china, and glass may not match, but their unity is a reflection of your decorative taste. Take your time in making selections, or acquire them over a period of years —you will live with them for a long time. And if your tastes change, feel free to reject, rejuvenate, or replace. Your favorite charity bazaar will welcome your outmoded tableware.

While silver adds beauty to your luncheon and dinner table and new gold-colored alloys add subtle glow, you may want to consider stainless-steel flatware for breakfast use, if only to avoid egg discoloration. And you will be smart to keep a stock of plastic forks and spoons on hand for picnics, portable meals, and drop-in crowds.

If you have sterling silver, you make extra work by using it only for company. Use it every day—washing prevents tarnish. The tiny scratches of daily use create a patina of subtle beauty.

Selection of china has changed markedly. While a bride used to yearn for two or more "sets" of dishes, it is more contemporary to mix and match artfully, keeping the dishes for each meal within a mood. The collector may build up a stock of soup bowls, dessert plates, cups and saucers, salad plates, or matching dinner service. These add interest and beauty to meals.

Fine china fuses delicate beauty and durability; stoneware and earthenware have rugged character. High-fired stoneware is more durable than earthenware; although chipable, low-fired earthenware keeps food hot—or keeps it cold—best of any ceramic ware. Stoneware rings when you tap it; earthenware gives forth a dull thunk. Basically, that's how you tell them apart.

Glass adds beauty of shape and form to a table, and good design is available in almost any price range. A formal table may be set with three or four different wine glasses, but for most uses, a universal stemmed glass with a fairly wide, deep bowl and simple design can serve for all wines. A basic collection of four glasses to cover most purposes would include a tall straight-sided tumbler or highball glass, a wide, chunky "old-fashioned" glass for cocktails or fruit juices, a short-stemmed glass for appetizer juices, sherry, or cocktails, and a wide, fairly large-footed all-purpose wine glass or goblet.

If wine is served in the goblet, it may be more interesting to use a different shape for water. Cordial or brandy glasses are high on the list if you entertain a lot and enjoy after-dinner drinks. Footed sherbets or low glass fruit or dessert plates are welcome additions.

Glass serving dishes enable the diner to see the food more easily. Footed glass cake plates in graduated sizes are adaptable to fruit arrangements, centerpiece decorations, and molded salads as well as their intended uses.

Basic tablesetting

Whether you use cloth or mats, the setting for an informal meal follows simple rules of logic.

All the flatware, up to the dessert course, is placed in the order in which it is to be used. If soup is to be served, soup bowls (or cups and saucers) are placed on the service plates and the soup spoons on the far right. If soup is served from a mug, place it to the upper right of the service plate. If you plan to serve cut-up fruit instead of soup, substitute teaspoons for the soup spoons; if your first course is to be salad or fish, put appropriate forks to the left of the luncheon or dinner forks, and omit the spoons.

At a very formal meal, butter plates are omitted. Always add salad forks if salad is to be served. To avoid last-minute servings of dessert utensils, the dessert spoon (and fork, if necessary) is placed above the service plate.

The breakfast table

Your first meal of the day may have little relation to the ordered pattern of tablesetting for a sit-down meal. Breakfast isn't likely to be leisurely if your family is typical, but breakfast can get the day off to a better start if a little extra thought is given to it. Set the table the night before. (You save time and motion if you do this while you're emptying the dishwasher.)

A bright, clear course is charted for a day that starts off with a meal set out on mats with colorful china and a simple centerpiece, bread and butter plates, marmalade or jam in a small pot, a favorite cheese, eggs, or cereal, piping hot coffee—ah, life can be beautiful!

On weekend mornings, make the most of breakfast. Serve a relaxed, beautiful meal with flowers and morning colors for mats. Use the bread and butter plates for popovers or hot rolls, your best coffee cups, your silver jam spoon. Make it a happy start for weekend meals, and some of the glow will last through an easy, pick-up lunch—on paper plates.

Serving pieces

The pieces in which you carry food to the table add to its attractiveness and appeal and can help keep hot foods hot, cold foods cold. Ovenware serving pieces that fit into attractive holders, or range-to-table cooking pans and chafing dishes, are convenient to use, and keep foods hot. A warming tray is convenient for keeping foods warm for second helpings.

Select a first course that can be on the table when guests come to the dining table. If you serve hot soup, have soup plates and a tureen ready, and ladle the first course as soon as guests are seated.

The formal dinner

Into even the most casual life a little formality must fall— as formal as white damask, taper candles, and a table set with large napkins folded into a rectangle or into a soft roll to show a monogram on service plates when guests are seated.

For a formal dinner, tables should be laid with white cloths, underlined by felt or mats, with matching napkins. (A large cloth needs two people for laying it properly.)

Flatware should be sterling silver, the best you have. Place it one inch from the edge of the table, each piece lining up at the base with the one next to it in a straight line. Do not hide the silver with the place plate. If the plate has a design, arrange it so that the design is toward the guest. The napkin, large satin damask, is folded on the place plate.

Allow plenty of space between guests—24 inches is the minimum standard.

What glass for which use?

- Water goblet is placed above the tip of the dinner knife.
- Sherry (for soup course) is to the right of the water goblet.
- Red wine or white for entrée is to the right of the sherry.
- Last glass to the right is for dessert wine, such as sauterne or champagne.

More often today, champagne or a single wine is served throughout the meal. Then, only a champagne glass or wine goblet is placed next to the water goblet or next to the plate if no water is served. Glasses are placed in order of their use above the knives. Each glass is removed with the course it has accompanied. The exception is the dessert wine glass, which remains throughout the fruit and demitasse. Only goblets are correct for formal dinners.

Host and hostess sit at opposite ends of the table, the hostess closest to the kitchen entrance. If you have a long table and few guests, seat the host and hostess opposite each other at the center of the table, grouping guests right and left, and leave the ends of the table unset.

"Don'ts" for proper tablesetting:

- Don't use bread and butter plates at a very formal dinner. No butter is served.
- Don't place mustard pots, chili sauce, or Worcestershire sauce on a formal table.
- Don't fail to place an adequate supply of salt and pepper on a formal table. It can be in individual sets in silver, porcelain, or crystal. If open salt containers are used, include tiny spoons.
- Don't make a display of silver. Place no more than three forks or three knives at a time. (Knife blades face the plate.)
- Place no more than one spoon at right of knives—a spoon for soup or melon. It is placed at right of knives.
- Don't forget diners work from the *outside* in toward the plate in selecting either knives or forks.
- Don't worry about a coffee spoon. At a really formal dinner, coffee is not served until the demitasse is carried in and spoons are placed on the saucers to the right of each handle.
- Don't place ash trays, cigars, or cigarettes on a formal table. Pass these around with the coffee.

Formal service

All service is from the kitchen and serving pieces are never set on the table. Four silver candlesticks are customary, one at each corner of an imaginary rectangle containing the centerpiece, a comfortable distance from the place plates. A large table may hold two candelabra spaced equidistant from the centerpiece on the long way of the table.

Although ash trays are not usually provided, there may be a small silver or porcelain tray at each place with two cigarettes lying horizontally on the tray and a small box or book of matches below it. Otherwise, cigars and cigarettes are passed with the coffee. If a butler is employed, he passes cigars and lights each as he places the ash tray to the right of the guest.

Dessert service

There is an element of do-it-yourself to the most formal dessert service. The dessert plate is set before the guests (sometimes with a half-filled finger bowl on a small doily). The dessert spoon is placed at the right of the plate, the dessert fork at the left.

The guest rearranges dessert service this way: Lift the doily and finger bowl together and set them down above the plate to the left. Place the spoon on the table to the right of the dessert plate, and the fork to the left. This leaves the dessert plate ready to receive the dessert.

Leave the finger bowl to the left of the plate above the fork. When dessert is removed, dip your fingers into it casually and wipe them on the napkin. Wipe your lips, too, if appropriate.

Centerpieces

For a formal dinner, a large flower arrangement is usual, sometimes supplemented with two smaller arrangements at the ends of a large table. The Williamsburg Virginians, however, never used anything in a centerpiece that wasn't edible, all arranged on beautiful pewter plates. The centerpiece may be garden vegetables, fresh green artichokes with purple eggplant, an epergne of lemons and limes stacked up formally and studded with lemon leaves.

Flowers may be simple—a single type such as roses or anemones arranged in graduated heights in a bowl, or an elaborate arrangement of varied flowers to set or carry out the color scheme for the party; nosegays at each place in cordial glasses. A tall arrangement should go at the back of a table against a wall.

For a less formal table a collection of odd candlesticks makes an unusual centerpiece. Have the tapers above eye level, in a range of colors and shapes. Vacation souvenirs make memorable centerpieces—sea shells, rocks, "found objects," alone or combined with other things. Fruit, vegetables, leaves, shrubbery, dried grasses, even winter's bare branches, are materials for the centerpiece that gets attention.

Place cards

Place cards may be used any time. If the hostess is seating more than eight at one table, she will find them helpful. Cards may be of almost any material, formal or whimsical. A creative hostess will make her own as an extension of her theme.

The easy way out

The amount of equipment required to serve a formal dinner is somewhat staggering. If you settle for the easy way and call in a caterer, meet with him and go over everything, down to the last demitasse spoon. Be as explicit as possible, and come to a minutely detailed understanding at your very first meeting. This is the way to get an intelligent estimate of cost and to have a party that runs smoothly without emergencies. Above all, don't surprise the caterer with last-minute changes. Determine with him how many helpers are needed, what happens if the party extends after midnight, who stays and how the rate is affected. A good caterer's crew should make no mistakes.

Buffets

The buffet wins hands down as a time-and-motion-saver, whether it is an informal late supper, more formal dinner, brunch, lunch, cocktail party, or outdoor barbecue. The efficiency-minded hostess welcomes it because:

- Setting up is simplified.
- Effective buffet dishes may be prepared in advance and reheated just before being served, or served cold.
- Guests need not be limited by the size of the dining table or number of chairs.
- Guests serve themselves.
- Fewer dishes are used for both serving and eating, and cleanup is simplified.

For the usual buffet, the dining table (or a flush door set on wood supports and covered with a pad and tablecloth) makes an effective space for the buffet spread. If possible, set up small card tables, each with a centerpiece and salt and pepper (and possibly a candle), or use individual stack tables so that guests can sit down to eat after they serve themselves.

Flatware will be dictated by the menu. Keep the menu simple—casseroles, stew, or cassoulet. The usual sliced turkey and ham are difficult to cut if tables are not provided.

Arrange your buffet table with a high centerpiece to one side at the back and an orderly flow of serving utensils and dishes, so that guests come to first things first. For example: plates, cutlery, and napkins; then rice; then curried lamb to go over the rice; condiments, vegetables, salad, rolls, butter, cheese, crackers. Your dessert may also serve as part of the centerpiece arrangement; a filled and scooped melon, a pyramid of cookies, a topiary tree of sweets. After guests help themselves to the main course (and come back for seconds), set out dessert plates, and pull the desserts forward.

At a "seated" buffet, the table or tables are set up with flatware. Guests serve their plates at the buffet table or sideboard, but do not carry silver or beverage. If the tables do not seat even numbers, and one half-empty table results, the host and hostess should go and sit at this table with the guests.

If there is a maid, she will clear and serve dessert and beverage. If not, guests are quite accustomed to doing this for themselves. It is good to continue to serve coffee after dessert, but the cups should be removed in a half-hour or so. The informality of the buffet, plus an organized dining-table setup, can be appropriate even for a black-tie party.

Napkin art

Napkins have come a long way in a short time. Colonial diners wiped their mouths on the corner of the tablecloth. Now napkins help to establish the mood and style of the table, add color accents and help mark special occasions. The paper napkin was the first major disposable table accessory to gain broad acceptance at all income levels. Whatever their material, napkins should be soft to the touch and absorbent. Colorful napkins may set off a flowered cloth; white napkins add a note of formality to the table. Inexpensive colored cotton kerchiefs make colorful napkins for informal meals or outdoor use.

If space is tight, fold the napkins in neat rectangles and place them on the dinner plate; or roll and place them above the plate with the dessert spoon. A simple fold is always in good taste.

Whatever the final shape, begin by folding a luncheon or standard napkin in quarters. For informal settings, for breakfast, lunch, afternoon tea or buffet, a triangular fold is practical. Place the corners away from the plate and leave the diagonal fold unpressed.

For a simple oblong fold, role over once more, lengthwise, after the napkin is in quarters. With the decorative corner at the lower left and facing outward, the napkin is placed at the left of the forks.

A very large damask napkin is folded in thirds, and then again, generally in thirds. For a long soft roll, it may be folded in half, and then rolled.

You may occasionally want to fold napkins decoratively for a special effect. In a Victorian setting, fold them as for pleated fans and set them in water goblets. Or for a Scandinavian effect, fold napkins into quarters with open points up.

Napkin rings, once the thrifty Victorian way to identify diners' napkins from meal to meal, now take on a decorative role. These may be colorful raffia, wood, or silver, and can help cut down on family laundry.

Napkin sizes

Dinner napkins	17 to 20 inches
Luncheon napkins	15 to 17 inches
Tea napkins	11 to 12 inches

Dinner is served

When the welcome words "dinner is served" are heard, whether the hostess says them herself or they are announced by a servant, she follows with, "Won't you come in, please."

The family knows the way to their seats, but if there are a few guests, places are pointed out; for a larger group, cards are appropriate. Alternate men and women in the seating arrangement, with female guest of honor to the host's right, male guest of honor to the hostess's right.

When a servant is available, food is brought in and shown first to the hostess and then served first to the lady guest of honor. After this, the service proceeds around the table counterclockwise, the host being served last. After the first three guests are served, it is proper to begin eating.

Although food is served from the left because it is easier for right-handed people to serve themselves that way, it is gracious to serve a southpaw from the right. Dishes are generally removed from the right, but may be taken from the left if that is more practical.

The real challenge to efficiency comes when the hostess serves alone—and manages a gracious, well-cooked meal without fluster.

The first step to simplified service begins with a first course on the table as guests sit down and continues with the main course on a serving cart, warm and ready to be served as guests finish.

After first-course plates are removed, dinner plates may be individually passed to the host, or a stack of warm dinner plates may be set before him to be filled with the main course from a serving casserole or from a platter on which he can carve the meat. He also serves the vegetables, and the hostess serves salad, bread, and butter. Each passes first to the lady on the host's right and then around the table. The host or a son serves the wine, standing and pouring at each place without lifting the glasses.

As an alternative, the table may be attractively set; after the first course, the main course is placed on a sideboard or serving cart from which guests help themselves.

After the main course, dishes are cleared and dessert and coffee served. It may simplify service if this is done in the living room, leaving the main course plates on the table to be cleared later.

If you are serving a crowd, desserts prepared in ready-for-the-table units are simplest to serve. These include individual tarts, pots de crème, and sherbet frozen in lemon or orange shells and served with a green leaf for garnish.

One of the triumphs of contemporary living is the easy, friendly flow of hospitality. An even flow of housekeeping and cooking enables a woman to welcome guests without panic, to say, "Come over for coffee and dessert any time," and mean it. Parties, as well as home meals, are often spontaneous happenings in which the pleasure is all the greater because it is unexpected.

For all its informality and casual service, however, snack food takes planning.

Stock a supply of canned nuts and dry nibbles, pickled vegetables and savory cheeses, crackers and thin-sliced bread. Popping corn provides both fun and ready refreshment. Pizza is handy in the freezer or as a mix. An ice-cube maker and reserve cubes in the freezer (even a reserve ice mold) make it easy to pour cold drinks to taste or to stir up a punch bowl.

For hot coffee on tap, you'll want a supply of regular coffee, some dark roast for after-dinner drinks, and decaffeinated coffee, perhaps in individual packets, for special tastes.

You'll want tea for the teapot, tea bags, and perhaps a spicy orange-scented brew over which to spend an evening of talk.

With a reserve cake in the freezer or tins of date-nut bread on the shelf, frosting in tubes, ice cream in reserve, and birthday candles in a box with food colors and decoration, you're ready even for an unexpected anniversary or birthday guest.

Disposable party settings

If you keep a reserve supply of paper plates and cups, clear plastic cups for cocktails, foam or plastic hot-drink cups for coffee or tea, you are prepared to take on a committee meeting or a whole Scout troop without even pausing for cleanup. A rubbish bag to collect debris does the cleanup trick.

Tea table tactics

The tea table, once a favorite exercise in afternoon entertainment, still functions well for large groups. Cover the table with a white or lace cloth. Arrange a centerpiece in the middle. Place complete tea service and cups at one end of the table; coffee service at the other. Place appropriate cups, saucers, and spoons near each. Small napkins, too. Arrange cakes, cookies, and small sandwiches on platters and pedestal plates between the two. Provide stacks of small plates for self-help. Delegate a hostess to serve at each end of the table. Guests gather at either end to receive their beverages. The hostess hands each a cup and saucer with spoon and napkin, and then guests circle the table to help themselves to accompanying cakes and sandwiches.

Parties in your life

A social history of man could be written in terms of his celebrations. From the earliest recorded wedding feasts—which were really times when the bridegroom's family fought off the bride's would-be rescuers—to contemporary outdoor weddings, parties have reflected the social sense, the concerns, and the joys of the time.

Your party lists may not run to hundreds, and your own living room may be far from a ballroom, but these seven elements of planning for interest and suspense make for a good party anywhere:

- Choose people for an interesting interplay of character and attitudes—but avoid sharply clashing personalities.
- Set a mood and a theme for your party, and carry out the theme in decor and food.
- Let guests in on your party plan in advance—they'll enjoy the occasion more.
- Be comfortable with what you have for equipment; augment, if necessary, with disposable ware.
- Make the most of color, design, and interest in your table setting and no one will question its cost.
- Set your table to reflect the warmth of your welcome, rather than cold correctness, and guests will be happier.
- Take advantage of easy serving techniques, including self-help at bar and buffet, and easy-serving dishes.
- Plan for ease of cleanup by leaving a bag or container in readiness for rubbish, the sink filled with soapy water in which to soak pans, utensils and dishes as they are cleared. Teflon-coated cookware will need no soaking before cleanup.
- Enjoy the parties in your life!

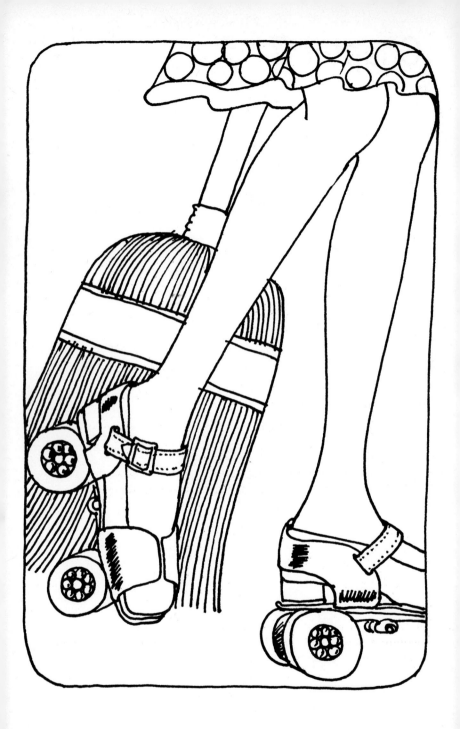

Chapter 7

How to clean up and quit the kitchen fast

The most important contribution yet for fast kitchen getaway is the introduction of Teflon nonstick finishes for pots and pans of all kinds—top-of-the-range cooking utensils, oven bakeware, and some small appliances, such as electric frypans and waffle bakers. Nonstick cooking means no-scour cleaning.

More than seventy manufacturers of kitchenware are now using Teflon coatings, applying them to aluminum, stainless steel, cast iron, porcelain, and even glass.

Cooking with Teflon-coated cookware

Before using a Teflon-coated utensil for the first time, wash it in hot, soapy water, rinse thoroughly, and dry. When you acquire a new skillet, griddle, or item of bakeware, it is a good idea to grease the nonstick surface lightly with cooking oil or shortening to "season" or precondition it. (Exception: the tubed angel-food-cake pan is never greased, because the batter must lightly cling to the sides of the pan during baking.)

Cooking with Teflon-coated pots and pans is no different from cooking with noncoated cookware. Extremely high heat, above 450° F., should be avoided, however. With too much heat, foods can burn, just as they can in uncoated pans. However, since the burned foods won't ordinarily stick to the slick Teflon finish, the pan is much easier to clean.

While the use of oil or grease is seldom necessary when cooking in nonstick pots and pans, some cooks prefer to use it for added flavor and as an aid to even browning. Light greasing of the Teflon finish is recommended when baking cakes (except angel food) and other foods containing sugar or fruit. Nonstick-coated cake pans also may be floured, if desired.

Wash nonstick cookware thoroughly in hot suds after each use. Because food slips out of the pans so easily, leaving little or no visible residue, it is easy to overlook a thin film of grease. If this film is allowed to build up, the finish may become stained and begin to lose some of its nonstick property. Either a plastic mesh pad or a sponge is excellent for washing nonstick pans. They should always be washed with a detergent, not just rinsed off with clear water and put away. If any food accumulates at all on a Teflon surface, it should be scrubbed off. To remove stubborn spots use a plastic mesh dishpad or the nylon side of the new "Combo" sponge-scrubber, which is nylon-surfaced on one side and cellulose sponge on the other. You may, of course, scour the *outside* of the pan. Teflon finishes are not affected by washing in an automatic dishwasher, although the exterior surfaces or other parts of some pans may be damaged or discolored. Follow directions of the cookware manufacturer.

You may want to minimize scratches on a Teflon finish by using a light touch when stirring with a metal spoon, or by using Teflon-coated utensils. It is wise to avoid cutting food with a sharp utensil in a coated pan. However, scratching is seldom a problem with pans labelled TEFLON II. This is a Du Pont certification mark which represents a coating system combining a "hard base" with Teflon finishes. TEFLON II certified wares offer outstanding scratch-resistance, so that metal tools can be used without fear of a badly marred finish.

If scratches do occur, no real damage has been done to the performance quality of a Teflon finish. Only its appearance has changed. Hairline scratches do not widen with continued use; if the coating has been applied properly, it will not peel off or lose its nonstick quality, nor will the food be affected in any way.

Prevent staining by washing well and avoiding the use of high heat. With long use, minor stains may appear, especially on light-colored Teflon finishes. These stains have little or no effect on the utensil unless they are allowed to build up. To lighten or eliminate them, stain removers developed specifically for Teflon are available. Or boil this mixture in the stained pan for 5 to 10 minutes: one cup water, a half-cup liquid bleach, two tablespoons baking soda. After this treatment, wash and recondition the pan with oil. Do not allow the stain remover solution to boil over, as it may damage the outside of the pan. Stain removers may bleach the pigments in a Teflon finish, but this will not lessen the nonstick quality.

The art of disposing

Cleanup time starts during meal preparation, as vegetable parings, eggshells, and other refuse collects, along with food packages and damp paper towels. Use the paper towels to keep the trimmings picked up, and keep a grocery bag or a waxed garbage bag handy. This same bag placed close to the cleanup center can serve for plate scrapings and used paper napkins when the table is cleared after the meal.

In some localities it is necessary to keep wet garbage separated from boxes, bottles, and cans in accordance with regulations. Drain wet garbage, and wrap it in layers of newspaper. Rinse cans and bottles so they won't attract insects and rodents.

Increasingly, food-waste disposers are becoming standard kitchen equipment. There are two types of electric food-waste disposers, the continuous-feed type that operates whenever a wall switch is thrown on, and the kind that must have the cover locked into position before it will start. Either kind must have a full stream of cold water turned on before it is started, and the water should be allowed to flush away all particles for a few seconds after the disposer has been stopped. Newer, heavier models can grind virtually any kind of food waste except bones too large to go into the drain opening. Melon rinds, corn cobs, and fruit cores should be broken or cut into pieces before they are dropped into the disposer. Celery, corn husks, pea pods, and other fibrous materials are fed gradually; they take longer to be flushed away. Raw bread dough, cold oatmeal, and any viscous food that clogs is added alternately with fruit and vegetable parings. Clam and oyster shells and other nonfood wastes must not be placed in the disposer. Glass, china, metal, string, cigarettes, especially filtertips, which mat the shredding ring, can necessitate a service call.

Some communities have prohibited disposers because it was thought the sewerage system would be overtaxed. In other communities, the installation of disposers in new residences is required by law.

Where do you set things down?

For streamlining cleanup, it's important to have room to set things down. If you don't have counter space on both sides of the sink, improvise extra space with a portable cart or a covering for the range top—anything to provide extra work surface. This is doubly important if other members of the family help clear the table.

Stack dishes at one side of the sink or in the sink itself. If dishes are greasy or sticky, they can be prerinsed. Soak pots and pans (except nonstick wares) if you have neglected to wash or soak them as you finished preparing the meal. Containers that have been used for raw starch, raw egg, cereal, milk, or cream should be rinsed or soaked in cold water; all others take hot water.

Collection depots for leftovers

While dishes are soaking in hot, sudsy water, put away leftover food. Here a forward-thinking homemaker can save herself a lot of motions and mileage. Some foods, like stew, are even better the second day. These can be stored in an oven-to-table dish, covered, and refrigerated. The next day, simply lift off excess fat, and reheat. Foods to be served cold can be scraped into smaller serving dishes and covered for the refrigerator. Combine other foods and convert them to new uses—leftover cheese, combined with anchovies, a chopped pickle, and a dash of cream makes a spread for canapes or sandwiches. Bits of meat and vegetables and their juices go into the classic *pot au feu* for soup stock. Employ putting-away time to prepare as much as possible for the next use of the food or utensil.

Washing dishes

How many times a day do you wash dishes? How much time does it take you? If you spend more than five hours a week washing dishes—and if you dislike it—you are typical. Studies show that dishwashing is the most disliked task in homemaking; and perhaps not so surprisingly, women who dislike it spend more time at it than women who can take it or leave it.

Speedy dishwashing takes two hands. The progression of work is from right to left. The left hand holds the plate while the right swabs it off. As the left hand puts the clean plate in the dish drainer, the right hand starts to rub the dish mop over the next plate—and the left hand picks it up out of the dish water. (This is reversed for left-handed people.) Keep "dirty" dishes stacked on the right. If desired, silver can soak in hot, sudsy water with the handles sticking out like a bouquet. Silver made after World War II isn't harmed by soaking the handles; other materials (except stainless steel and laminated

---

CLEAN-UP EFFICIENCY HINT: To save time in cleaning measuring cups and spoons, first measure dry ingredients and put them on waxed paper; then use the same cups and spoons for measuring liquid ingredients.

wood) may be harmed; flatware manufactured prior to World War II may come uncemented. Do not soak cutlery; all knives, including stainless steel knives, should be washed and dried after each use and returned to their drawer or magnet holder.

Choose any order for dishwashing that is most convenient. If the pans and cooking utensils have soaked, it may be advantageous to have them out of the way swiftly. If the dinner plates have soaked during dessert, that might be the place to start. If it's been a large dinner party with several wines, it would be best to have the stemware out of the way first.

The classic order for hand-washing dishes, however, is crystal and glassware first, then silver, dishes, platters, pots and pans, changing the sudsy water as necessary. Some homemakers wear rubber gloves to enable them to use hotter water. Long-handled sponges and brushes help keep hands out of water. For those who wash dishes by hand and do not use gloves, new detergents and soaps are designed for "gentleness." If your hands are sensitive, it may pay to find the brand that works best for you— or use those rubber gloves.

Air drying is more efficient than towel drying and more sanitary. If dishes drain overnight, they can be covered with a towel and carried to the dining area in the drainer to set the table for breakfast.

Once you start your cleanup countdown, stick to it; continuity is important. As the dish drainer is filled, put other things to soak, and use this time to wipe off countertops, to tend to spills at the range, to pick up crumbs with the carpet sweeper, and to straighten up the dining room. If necessary, use two dish drainers.

When the dishes are done, scour the sink, and rinse it. If the scouring powder contains a bleach, this can be left in the dish cloth or sponge overnight once in a while, for a mild bleaching action.

Dishwashing implements

The following tools and supplies belong at the sink center:

- Plate scraper
- Paper towels
- Rubber, neoprene, or other household gloves (optional)
- Cellulose sponge with a nylon side for scrubbing, or brush
- Bottle brush or other brushes (optional)
- Protective rubber or plastic mats for sink bottom and double sink divider (optional)
- Drain tray (if sink is counter-sunk)
- Dish drainer
- Dishwashing detergent
- Silver polish
- Metal polish
- Ammonia
- Scouring powder
- Dish towels
- Hand lotion

Automatic dishwashers

A dishwasher washes dishes cleaner and more quickly than anyone can by hand. The bacterial count on dishwasher-washed dishes is virtually zero; the time spent scraping the dishes and loading the machine, compared to washing dishes by hand, is the difference between an easy chore and a real job.

Dishwashers can be permanently built-in, free-standing, or portable. In addition, so-called "convertible" portable machines can have their casters removed so that they can be built in under a standard kitchen cabinet top. Check between front-loading and top-opening models. Front-loading models take more floor space when the door is open, but when closed, the top is usable as a work surface. Top-loading models must be cleared off to open.

There are several ways in which the impeller distributes the water; know your system in order to stack dishes most effectively. Some automatic dishwashers have cycles for heavily and lightly soiled loads, as well as for normal loads.

A rinse-and-hold cycle is convenient for rinsing off soil that might dry on and for dishes collected to be washed once a day or whenever the dishwasher is filled. In some machines, the drying cycle can be used as a plate warmer. Dishwashers, with their superior cleaning power and heat, are thought to be a factor in curbing colds and other communicable family illnesses.

In most dishwashers, no particular preparation of dishes is required except to remove loose food waste. Some models have flush-away drains; others have a pump that grinds up soft food and flushes it away.

It pays to read the use-and-care booklet that comes with each machine; it shows the machine's preferred loading pattern. Dishes must be loaded correctly for the water jets to reach all surfaces. There is a basket for silver, and a pattern is usually recommended for loading pots and pans. One manufacturer maintains that burned-on spots can be removed in the dishwasher, but most stubborn and burned-on spots require hand care.

There are many dishwasher detergents. It is essential to use one formulated for automatic dishwashing, and it is wise to ask your dealer which brands give the best results in your area. If spotting is a problem because of the mineral content of the water, a wetting agent may be added either by an automatic dispenser for the purpose or manually. Always use detergent in the amount and in the manner recommended by the manufacturer. Too much interferes with the washing action and can spill over. If not introduced properly, as engineered by the manufacturer, it can cause faulty washing.

The dishwasher is the great ally of fast cleanup and getaway families because it hides dirty dishes. Fill the detergent cup when the first dirty dishes are deposited; if the detergent cup is open and empty, this informs any member of the family that clean dishes are to be put away—or ready to use to set the table.

Arrange dish storage close to the dishwasher since, after all, dishes are taken only to and from the storage cabinet, the eating area, and the dishwasher.

Tips to reduce breakage

- Handle only a few pieces at a time. Handle cut glass one piece at a time.
- Avoid overcrowding either in dishpan, drainer, or dishwasher.
- Avoid the excess weight of high stacks of plates or platters.
- Use wire-covered accessories for stacking cups, for dividing deep shelves. They are specially designed for these uses.
- Use trays for setting and clearing the table. Teach children to carry small loads on trays. Line a slippery tray with a dish towel to keep dishes from sliding.
- Avoid sudden extremes in temperatures. Allow water tumblers to warm up after ice water is emptied before washing. Temper thin or thick glass with warm water, then with hot rinses before introducing hot foods or liquids. This is particularly important when you are washing vacuum bottle liners.
- Avoid setting hot glass or hot ceramic cooking utensils on a wet sink or any cold or wet surface until they have cooled.

- Carpet the kitchen for softness underfoot. This effectively reduces all kitchen clatter and appreciably reduces breakage. The new rubber-backed kitchen carpeting of long-wearing continuous-filament nylon enhances kitchen decor; you simply sponge off spilled liquids.

To scour or not to scour

Not long ago there was no choice; anyone who cooked and kept house scoured pots and pans. Teflon nonstick finishes for pans are among the world's great boons to women; slick surfaces eliminate scouring and minimize scrubbing. The dramatic appeal of these finishes is revolutionizing kitchen pan cabinets and washing techniques across the country. Usually, washing a nonstick pan after cooking is a simple matter of a few swishes with a sudsy sponge or cloth and a quick rinse. Even sticky or burned foods that cling to corners are easily whisked away. A periodic scrubbing with a nylon pad or the nylon side of a "Combo" sponge-scrubber will keep grease stains from building up. Scouring is never needed—and, in fact, will mar the finish.

Noncoated utensils, however, still require some scouring and frequent scrubbing. Here are some tips:

Aluminum and aluminum-clad utensils. These take on a dark film from cooking alkaline foods, from boiling water, and from exposure to cooking gas—unless they have nonstick interiors. This film can be removed by cooking acid foods such as tomatoes, rhubarb, and tart apples in the pan. Neither the pan nor the food is harmed by the discoloration, but the pans aren't as attractive as most homemakers want them to be. A heavy discoloration can be removed by boiling two teaspoons of cream of tartar to a quart of water, and then it can be scoured away with a nylon-faced sponge and scouring powder. Regular use of such a sponge at dishwashing time keeps pans shiny without heavy scrubbing.

Stainless steel. This requires little more than suds-and-water care. If it sometimes takes on a slight film that can be removed with scouring powder and a nylon-faced sponge. Bluish heat marks can be minimized with scouring powder or special stainless-steel cleanser, but metal discoloration from overheating is usually permanent. Plastic mesh or stainless-steel pads should be used for scouring.

Copper. May be polished with a special copper polish or a cut lemon dipped in salt, or with vinegar and salt. Rinse thoroughly and dry immediately.

Glass and porcelain. These should *never* be scoured, since a surface scratched by scouring becomes harder to clean, but difficult spots may need scrubbing with a plastic mesh ball. Baked-on grease may need soaking.

Black cast-iron. Some people never wash noncoated cast-iron pots and skillets, but wipe them out after usage. Other people consider this unsanitary. Unfortunately, detergents remove much of the "seasoning" from the pores of wiped-only cast-iron pots, causing food to stick more easily. A damp cast-iron pot, if not enamel-clad, will rust. It can never be left to drain dry. You must wipe a cast-iron pot immediately after washing and set it in a warm oven or on a warm burner to dry thoroughly. Coat with a film of cooking oil and place in 350° F. oven. Allow it to cool in the oven with the heat turned off. Remove excess oil with paper towel.

First aid for the pot burned black

A cooking utensil burned black and exuding smoke and fumes is a crisis in anybody's kitchen. Stifle the impulse to flood the offending utensil with water. That can result in a shattered glass or enameled surface, and a badly warped bottom in any other material. Open the window, turn on the exhaust fan and just let the pot sit there.

If flames are shooting up, smother them with baking soda. The soda produces a blanket of carbon-dioxide gas, and the fire dies of oxygen starvation.

When the pan has cooled, boil some water in it, with or without detergent, and scrape away the burned crust with a rubber scraper or wooden spoon. Repeat if necessary, and polish with a nylon-faced sponge and a sprinkle of scouring powder.

Occasional special care

Silver. The best care you can give silver is to use it every day. The next best thing is to rotate it so that all of the pieces develop the same beautiful luster. This is easy to do with solid flatware, especially when there is a dishwasher, but less easy to do with hollow ware. Seldom-used silver should be polished and stored away in airtight wrappings (plastic wrap

is excellent for this), or in tarnish-proof bags or chests. Moth balls help retard tarnish.

Egg tarnishes silver, and salt corrodes it if left in contact too long. Light tarnish can be removed with a rough cloth or with treated paper at dishwashing time or whenever it is noticed. Occasionally, a thorough polishing with silver polish and a soft cloth is in order. Polish lengthwise, always in the same direction, never in a circular motion. Use cotton-tipped sticks to follow the crevices. Remove candle wax from candlesticks with warm water or carbon tetrachloride, but do not immerse or soak hollow ware candlesticks.

In an earlier generation when the good silver was used only on state occasions, it was customary in some households to separate the knives, forks, and spoons for washing to minimize scratching. Silversmiths say that all the minute little scratches are incurred in the first two weeks of use. It is the myriad little scratches that make up the attractive patina of silver in a home, as contrasted to the mirror finish it has when it comes from the store.

Glassware and crystal. If a great deal of decorative crystal or cut glass is to be washed, extend the draining surface by placing the pieces upside down to drain on towels. A little ammonia in the rinse water or a few drops of wetting agent will prevent spots. A few tablespoons of dishwashing detergent in hot water will soak even oily city soil away without scrubbing. However, detergent is hard on hands, and glassware must be handled with gloves, even if gloves feel awkward to wear. Glass will dry clear when rinsed in hot water and drained except in very-hard-water areas.

Metal-trimmed glasses discolor with ammonia or strong dishwasher detergent, and its use should be avoided. If they are discolored, polish gently with a rouge cloth.

Cloudiness in a vinegar cruet can be removed by soaking in ammonia or dishwasher detergent and hot water.

Spot treatment for kitchen floors

Almost anything that falls to the floor needs immediate attention; otherwise it will be tracked over a broader area. If it is dry, you'll want to pick it up or sweep it up. If it's sugar, salt, or flour, the quickest solution is to plug in the vacuum cleaner; an electric broom is very convenient for kitchen use. Broken glass should be swept up with a broom first; then use wet paper towels to pick up tiny splinter fragments.

Wet spills may be picked up with a damp sponge or damp paper towel, or soaked up with towels or newspapers. The remaining stain then should be swabbed. Grease spills—in fact, all spills—come out more satisfactorily if they are treated soon after the accident. Immediately blot the grease with dry paper towel, then rub it with a sudsy sponge. If time is precious, finish removing it after the meal. If you drop a raw egg on the floor, don't chase it; cover it with salt, and scoop it onto a dust pan or any flat surface. Wipe up acid foods and deep-colored stains immediately, being especially careful to remove them from appliances and cabinets.

If any of these first-aid treatments removes the wax on a

resilient floor covering, the wax can be patched without doing the whole floor.

Rubber-backed, 100 percent continuous-filament nylon kitchen carpet gives new ease underfoot and requires even less care in the kitchen than a shiny floor surface. Spills can be picked up or washed up. Occasionally, the carpet sweeper or the vacuum cleaner is needed after a meal, depending on the traffic and the wear and tear. A damp sponge soaks up liquids. The surface can be brightened with an occasional swabbing with a damp sponge mop; nylon gives up stains easily, since the fiber doesn't absorb them. In place of waxing and polishing, nylon kitchen carpet requires routine shampooing, which is done in a jiffy with solution and applicator for this purpose. It takes a very few minutes once every month or two, and the carpet dries overnight. A burn or other serious spot damage is easily remedied by removing a circle of carpet with a special new scriber and popping in an identical disk of fresh carpet.

Summing up

Housemaking today is pretty much "doing your own thing." If storage is a problem, you can plan your possessions to serve several purposes. For example, a wide, all-purpose goblet is acceptable for any wine, for fruit cup, for parfaits, for Irish coffee in the living room after dinner.

If you're entertaining more people than your furnishings can serve, rent glassware; or use the handsome throw-away plastic cups or glasses similar to those the airlines use. The long list of throw-aways gets longer every day—"linens" and dishes, even paper party dresses. One New York restaurant now serves its fabulous chocolate mousse in edible chocolate dishes.

Considerably closer than the horizon are convenience foods in edible containers that can be heated on slick surfaces—the ultimate in kitchen cleanup of the future—if, indeed, you have a kitchen at all as we now know it.

Woman's work is never done, the adage had it. As the working world, in which women are now some twenty million participants, moves toward a shorter work week, with more time for leisure activities, will the homemaking function keep pace? Servants have disappeared from the home scene. Appliances, simplifying effort and saving time in homemaking tasks, are today's servants.

Whatever comes in the way of easier-to-use, time-telescoping, effort-saving tools for food service, one piece of equipment can and will accommodate to changing technology for the greater enjoyment of life. *You.*

Glossary of
cooking terms

BAKE To cook by dry heat in an oven. Called "roasting" when applied to meat.

BARBECUE To roast slowly on a gridiron or a spit over coals, or under an oven broiler, usually basting with a seasoned sauce.

BASTE To moisten food while it is cooking by spooning on liquid or fat.

BATTER A mixture of flour and liquid, usually combined with other ingredients, as in baked products. The mixture is of such consistency that it may be stirred with a spoon and is thin enough to pour or drop from a spoon.

BEAT To make a mixture smooth; with an electric mixer, eggbeater, or mixing spoon (or wire whip), to lift a mixture rapidly over and over, bringing bottom ingredients to surface and mixing evenly.

BLANCH To preheat briefly in boiling water or steam. Blanching in cooking is used to aid in removal of skins from fruits, nuts, and vegetables. In food preservation, to inactivate enzymes and shrink some foods for canning, freezing, or drying. Vegetables are blanched in boiling water or steam; fruits are blanched in boiling fruit jars, syrup, water, or steam.

BLEND To combine two or more ingredients thoroughly.

BOIL To cook food in boiling liquid in which bubbles constantly rise to surface and break (212° F. at sea level). Once liquid boils, lower heat until just high enough to maintain bubble formation, as slow boiling is just as effective as rapid boiling.

BRAISE   To brown meat slowly and well on all sides in a little hot fat, about 15 to 20 minutes. Season, add a little water or other liquid, cover and simmer over low heat until tender. Braising is a method used for less tender meats.

BREAD   To coat with crumbs of bread or other food; or coat with crumbs and then with diluted, slightly beaten egg or cream or other thick liquid, and again with crumbs before cooking.

BROIL   To cook under the heat of a broiler or over hot coals or between two heated surfaces.

BRUSH   With pastry brush, to cover lightly with fat or slightly beaten egg white, cream, or other liquid.

CANDIED   When applied to fruit, fruit peel or ginger, food is cooked in a heavy sugar syrup until plump, then drained and dried. When applied to sweet potatoes and carrots, food is cooked in sugar and syrup. Also called "crystallized" food.

CARMELIZE   To melt granulated sugar over medium heat, stirring constantly until it forms a golden brown syrup.

CHILL   To place in refrigerator or other cold place until cold.

CHOP   Using knife, food chopper, or chopping board with knife, to cut up food as recipe directs. (See DICE, CUBE, MINCE.)

COAGULATE   To change from a fluid state to a thickened jelly, curd, or clump.

COAT   Thin outer covering of flour or flour mixture or crumbs, easily applied by shaking (as pieces of chicken) or rolling in flour or sugar, as directed, until coated; or with sifter, to sprinkle with flour or sugar, as directed, until coated.

COOL   To let stand at room temperature until no longer warm to touch.

CREAM   To work one or more foods until soft and creamy, using a spoon, wooden paddle, spatula, or beater; most frequently applied to mixing or blending fat and sugar together. Also applied to foods cooked in, or served with, a white sauce.

CUBE   Cut into small cubes, about ½ inch in diameter, unless otherwise specified.

CUT   To divide food materials with a knife or scissors.

CUT IN   To distribute solid fat in dry ingredients by chopping with knives or pastry blender until finely divided.

DASH   Less than ⅛ teaspoon of an ingredient, usually a spice.

DEEP-FAT-FRYING THERMOMETER   Thermometer specifically designed for deep frying to determine exact temperature of fat or oil; may be a deep-fat thermometer or combination deep-fat and candy thermometer. No other method of checking temperature is as reliable.

DEEP FRY   Method of cooking in which fat or oil is used in large enough quantity to cover food completely.

DEHYDRATION   A method of food preservation whereby most of the water from a food is removed by mechanical process.

DEHYDRO-FREEZING   A process of food preservation which combines dehydration and freezing. Both weight and bulk in packaging are reduced in the process.

DICE   Cut into very small cubes, about ½ inch in diameter.

DISSOLVE   Mix dry substance with liquid until in solution.

DOT   Scatter small bits of butter or margarine, or other ingredient, over surface of food.

DOUGH   Mixture of flour and liquid, usually with other ingredients added.

DREDGE   To sprinkle or coat with flour or other fine substances.

EMULSIFY   To make into an emulsion. When small drops of one liquid are finely dispersed in another liquid, an emulsion is formed. The drops are held in suspension by an emulsifying agent, which surrounds each drop to form a coating.

FOLD IN   To combine ingredients by using two motions, one which cuts vertically through the mixture and across the bottom, the other which turns over by bringing mixture up and across the top.

FREEZING   A method of preserving food by chilling it very rapidly at a low temperature (preferably −10° F. or below) and maintaining it at a temperature below 0° F.

FRICASSEE   To cook by braising. Usually applied to fowl, veal, or rabbit cut into pieces.

FRY   To cook in fat. When cooking in a small amount of fat, also called sauté or pan-fry; when cooking in a deep layer of fat, also called deep-fat frying.

GLACE   To coat with a thin sugar syrup glaze. When used for pies and certain types of bread, the mixture may contain thickening, but is not cooked to such a concentrated form; or a glace may be uncooked.

GRATE   To rub a food against a grater to produce fine, medium, or coarse particles, as required.

GREASE   To rub lightly with butter, margarine, shortening, or salad oil.

GRILL   To cook by direct heat; also a utensil or appliance used for such cooking.

GRIND   To reduce to fine particles by crushing or putting through a food chopper.

KNEAD   To manipulate with a pressing motion accompanied by folding and stretching.

LARD   To lay strips of salt pork or bacon on top of, or in gashes in, fish or meat to prevent dryness in roasting.

LUKEWARM   Approximately 95° F. Lukewarm liquids or food sprinkled on the wrist will not feel warm. Same as tepid.

MARINATE   To let food stand in a marinade liquid, usually an oil-acid (vinegar) or other thick sauce.

MELT   To place an ingredient or a food in a small pan, dissolve it to liquid over hot water, or over lowest heat, or in warm oven.

MICROWAVE   A very short electromagnetic wave of high-frequency energy produced by the oscillation of an electric charge. Time required for cooking food with microwave energy is dramatically short.

MINCE   To chop until fine with food chopper or knife.

MIX   To combine ingredients in any way that effects a distribution.

PAN-BROIL   To cook uncovered in a lightly greased or ungreased skillet. Fat is poured off as it accumulates.

PAN-FRY   To cook in a small amount of fat.

PARBOIL   To boil briefly until partially cooked in water or other liquid.

PARCH   To brown by means of dry heat; applied to grains such as corn.

PARE   To cut off the peel or outside covering.

PASTEURIZATION   The partial sterilization of a liquid at a temperature sufficient to destroy objectionable organisms without major chemical change to the substance being pasteurized.

PEEL   To strip off the outside covering.

PIT   To remove pit or seed, as from prunes.

POACH   To cook in a hot liquid, using precautions to retain shape of food.

POT-ROAST   Term applied to cooking large cuts of meat by braising. (*See* BRAISE.)

PREHEAT   To heat oven to desired baking temperature before putting in food.

PUREE   To press through fine sieve or food mill, or to reduce to a liquid in a blender.

RECONSTITUTE   To restore concentrated foods to their normal state, usually by adding water.

REHYDRATION   To soak, cook, or use other procedures to restore water lost during drying process.

RENDER   To free fat from connective tissue at low heat.

ROAST   To cook uncovered in hot air. Usually done in an oven, but occasionally in ashes, under hot coals, or on heated stones.

SAUTE   To brown or cook in a small amount of fat.

SCALD   To heat milk to just below the boiling point (when tiny bubbles form at edge). Sometimes refers to dipping certain foods in boiling water, as in blanching.

SCALLOP   To bake food (usually cut in pieces) with a sauce or other liquid. The food and sauce may be mixed together or arranged in alternate layers in a baking dish, with or without a topping of crumbs.

SCORE   To make shallow slits or gashes with a sharp knife.

SEAR   To brown surface of meat quickly over high heat.

SEASON   To sprinkle with salt and pepper or other spices or flavors to suit taste.

SHALLOW-FRY   To fry in fat, 1½ inches in depth, heated to the same temperature as for deep-fat frying.

SIFT   To put through flour sifter or fine sieve.

SIMMER   To cook in a liquid just below the boiling point, at temperature range of 185° F. to 210° F. Bubbles form slowly and collapse below the surface.

SINGE   To hold over a flame to burn off all hairs or feathers; refers particularly to poultry.

SKEWER   To hold in place by means of slender metal or wooden sticks.

SLIVER   To cut or split into long, thin pieces.

SNIP   With shears, to cut into small pieces.

SOLUTION   A uniform liquid blend containing a solute (as salt) dissolved in the liquid.

STEAM   To cook in steam with or without pressure, or steam may be applied directly to the food, as in a pressure cooker.

STEEP   To allow a substance to stand in liquid just below the boiling point for the purpose of extracting flavor, color, or other qualities.

STERILIZE   To destroy organisms in a food, usually at a high temperature, with steam, boiling liquid, or hot air.

STEW   To simmer in a small quantity of liquid.

STIR   To blend with a circular motion in widening circles until all ingredients are well mixed.

THICKEN   To increase density by using a thickening agent such as flour or cornstarch.

TOAST   To brown by means of dry heat.

TOSS   To mix lightly.

WARM   A food temperature of 105° F.

WHIP   To beat rapidly to incorporate air and produce expansion. Generally applied to cream, eggs, and gelatin mixtures.

Index

Centerpieces, 144–145
Ceramic sinks, 10
Ceramic tile, 18, 22, 24
Cheese, 131
Chickens, 78–79
  storage of, 97–98
China, 138–139
Chocolate, 132
Citrus fruits, rinds of, 92
Clabber, 130
Clams, freezing, 104–105
Cleaning up, 152–168
  broiler pans, 11
  enameled sinks, 19
Cleavers, 57
Cocoa, 132
Coconut, 132
Coffee, storage of, 89
Coffee makers, 46
Cold center, 6
  planning, 12–13
Cold storage at home, 115
Colonial Stores, 61
Colors, 19–22
Comfort, 121
Condensed milk, 130
Confectioners sugar, 127
Convenience foods, 63
Cookbooks, using, 121–123
Cooker-fryers, 47
Cookies
  freezing, 108
  storage of, 92
Cooking center, 6
  planning, 11–12
Copper, scouring, 163
Cork tile, 24
Corn meal, 126
Corn syrup, 128
Cornell University, 34
Cornstarch, 127
Corridor kitchens, 8
Counters, 15–18
Coverings, 19–24
Crab, freezing, 105
Cracked wheat, 127
Cranberry relish, 113
Cream, 77, 130–131
Cream puffs, 114
Crystal, special care, 166
Cupcakes, 122

Dairy products, 83, 129–132
  buying, 77–78
  freezer storage time, 101
  storage of, 95
Defrosting, 39–41
Design-your-own-island kitchen, 8–9
Dessert molds, 51
Dessert service, 144
Dishwashers, 42–43, 159–160
  plate-warming cycle, 42
Dishwashing, 157–161
  breakage, 161–162
  implements for, 158–159
Disposable party settings, 150
Disposers, 43–44, 155–156
Drink mixers, 45
Drop-in range, 33
Dry milk, 130
Ducks, 78
Dutch ovens, 47

Eating center, 13–14
Eggs, 83
  buying, 77–78
  freezer storage time, 101
  freezing, 107
  storage of, 94–95
Electric frypans, 46, 47
Electric knives, 57
Electric toasters, 46
Electric warming trays, 47
Enamel sinks, 10
Evaporated milk, 130
Everyday tablesetting, 136–137
Eye-level range, 33

Farina, 127
Fats, 82, 83, 129
  storage, 90–91
Federal Standard of Identity, 69
Fish, 78
  freezing, 104
  storage of, 97–98
Flatware, 146
Floor covering, 23–24
Flour, 83
  storage of, 88
  varieties of, 125–126
Food-preparation center, 5
Foods
  commercial can sizes, 70